Here's to you
(1935

We leave Frank Robinson the first image and last words of this issue. Shown here in his rookie year, he graced the cover of *Sport Literate's* "20th Anniversary Issue." For a bittersweet salute to the promise of his youth, check out Jerry Judge's poem on the last page.

Photo courtesy of the National Baseball Hall of Fame Library, Cooperstown, New York.

L

Inside Sausage

—

William Meiners

I may have mashed together two clichés in this title with the notions of "inside baseball" and "how the sausage gets made." But as recently I laid awake, awaiting the whispered breaths of a CPAP machine to make a surrealistic swirl of my dreams, I thought I'd write about how a *Sport Literate* issue comes together. If that sounds like cheering on drying paint, I'd jump to the poetry and essays to follow. That's why we print this pub in the first place.

We publish what we like. An unremarkable admission that I may have stated previously, perhaps in these pages. Somethings we like a lot. Some tickled us just enough to warrant a small assault on trees. Still others I may look back on, wondering why we liked *that* so much. That's not a slam on any contributing writers and poets. I won't like reading this in two months.

For their shared heartfelt words we pay contributors with two copies of the journal. And in my correspondence with them, I dangle discounted copies of more issues. By the way, if you've read this far, you should subscribe, or re-subscribe, or surprise that red-headed kid from your high school algebra class with an SL subscription. He could be a disgruntled red-headed man by now. Or a distinguished balding one. Maybe he'd like some honest reflections on life's leisurely diversions.

But before that redhead walked in I was going to talk about how an issue comes together. Like this one. We accept essays and poems we like. Have I established that? Some submissions are backlogged, resulting in a collection with 17 poets. Then we look for particular pairings (see Table of Contents). We're bookended by baseball — by two Bills focused on Yankee pinstripes. William Loizeaux leads us off and Bill Gruber takes us home. In between diamond reflections that include a virtual starting rotation, we've got a bicycling section built by two, a trio of runners, poetry from three hoopsters and two hockey fans, a musical golfer, two outdoor enthusiasts, and a slew of fighters. Tennis fans and non-racists will especially enjoy Markham Johnson's poem.

We've called this issue "Spring Broke 2019" because it's an old joke. A joke I've shared in winter semesters of Academic Writing in classrooms filled with the hatted heads and stony faces of the college freshmen not heading south for Spring Break. By "stony faces" I mean they were high on dope. Besides, in a Michigan mid-winter March (three points for alliteration), spring's arrival is hopelessly delayed, as if stuck in some sort of debtors' prison. Plus, we're broke. Always have been. See paragraph three about subscriptions to help keep this small press afloat.

There is some good news, however, in this discontented writing. I'm excited about our new publishing partnership with Mission Point Press out of Traverse City. From the layout, courtesy of California designer Bob Deck, to closer-to-home marketing efforts, MPP could put us on the Michigan map. From Chicago through a decade and a half at Purdue to the aforementioned middle Michigan, I've brought *Sport Literate* (with a lot of help from my friends in the masthead) to this particular middle age. Maybe we just can't quit each other.

———

William Meiners, the founding editor of *Sport Literate*, works as a freelance writer in Mount Pleasant, Michigan.

Billy Jo Bob: Growing up, people (mostly family) called me Bob, or Bobby, all the time. But I'm just a Bill, a nickname sometimes carelessly tossed at my brother Bob. And my father (also errantly called Bill because of his own father) often joked, "I'm a Bob with one 'o'." For the longest time, I tried to dig up an old picture of my dad to put in each *Sport Literate*. That's him at my wedding with my wife Joellen and my brother-in-law Bill. I know, it's complicated. Lots of Bobs and Bills. With my father no longer in the picture, we get a kick out of our son James (in utero in this photo) sometimes referring to Bill as Grandpa Bill. And his wife, my sister, as Grandpa Peggy. That Bill, incidentally, is the nicest guy I know. Robert, William, or otherwise.

Sport Literate

Volume 11, Issue 2

William Meiners
EDITOR

Frank Van Zant
POETRY EDITOR

Nicholas Reading
ASSISTANT EDITOR

Brian McKenna
ASSISTANT EDITOR

Glenn Guth
MOUTHPIECE

Bob Deck
GRAPHIC DESIGNER

Erin Ingram
WEB DESIGNER

Barney Haney and Molly Meiners
SOCIAL MEDIA SPECIALISTS

Steve Mend
MULTIMEDIA MAN

Kindle Digital Printing
PRINTER

MISSION POINT PRESS

Published by Mission Point Press
2554 Chandler Road
Traverse City, Michigan 49696

ISBN: 978-1-950659-00-5
ISSN: 1080-3247

Printed in the United States of America
Available for individual purchase at Amazon.com
For bulk orders, contact Doug Weaver at doug.missionpointpress@gmail.com; or by phone: 231-421-9513; or on the web at www.MPPDistribution.com.

Sport Literate™ features creative nonfiction, poetry, and interviews. Individual subscription rates are $20 for two issues (U.S. domestic only). Library and institution subscriptions are available for $30 for two issues. Subscriptions available through our website: www.sportliterate.org.

Correspondence can be sent to our Michigan headquarters.
Sport Literate
William Meiners
1422 Meadow Street
Mount Pleasant, MI 48858

We welcome all submissions of poetry and creative nonfiction (personal essays, literary journalism, travel pieces, etc.) that fall within our broad view of "sport." We don't knowingly publish fiction. Find contributor guidelines and the Submittable online submission tool on our website: www.sportliterate.org.

SUPPORT

Thanks to all who've supported *Sport Literate* through nearly 25 years. As we wrap this second and final issue of Volume XI, we'll hit up supporters to help build Volume XII. To continue supporting this award-winning small press endeavor, please make a tax-deductible donation to one of the categories below. Here's our current lineup:

Franchise Players $500
Mick and Kris Meiners, Anonymous (in memory of Bob and Eileen Meiners)

Pinch Hitters $100
Michael Burke, Patrick and Beth Gavaghan, John Girardi, Glenn and Kathleen Guth, Doug and Courtney Howie, Lalli-Steinberg Charitable Foundation, Lance Mason, Steve and Lisa Mend, Virginia Mend, Karl and Barb Meyer, Kevin and Susan Olehnik, Kenny and Judy Skarbeck, Mark Wukas

Bench Warmers $66
Terry Luctherhand, Bill and Peggy Roach, Augusto and MaryEllen Sarrias, Nora, Avery, and Julianna Sarrias, J.D. Scrimgeour

Pint-Size Publications

Sport Literate falls under the umbrella of Pint-Size Publications, a nonprofit corporation. Donations made payable to *Sport Literate* may be mailed to the address above, or donate online at www.sportl⬛

Spring Broke 2019　　SPORT **Literate**　　Volume 11, Issue 2

TABLE OF CONTENTS

WHO'S ON FIRST

8　William Loizeaux　　*Sin and Baseball*

SL BICYCLING

20　Michael Kula　　*How to Repair a Bicycle*

26　Laura Madeline Wiseman　*Helmet*
　　　　　　　　　　　　　　　Trail Cycler's Inn at Al's Place
　　　　　　　　　　　　　　　Road Flare

SL RUNNING

30　Cinthia Ritchie　　*Random Notes from a Summer of*
　　　　　　　　　　　　Alaskan Trail Running

34　Kara Thom　　*Surprising*

36　Scott F. Parker　　*Five Running Shorts*

SL BASKETBALL

40　Jim Daniels　　*Air Ball*

42　Barry Peters　　*Charlie, Larry, and Sparrow: A Triptych*

43　David Evans　　*At the Health Club*

SL FIGHTERS

44　Will Stenberg　　*Battling Battalino*
　　　　　　　　　　　Pete Herman
　　　　　　　　　　　Beau Jack

48　Justina Elias　　*A Deep, Sweet Hurt*

56　M.G. Ste　　*Boxing*

58　Eric　　*Our Hall of Fame*

61　　　　*Fairbanks 1980*

6　　　*Tennis Whites at Booker T. Washington*

SL SKATES

64	**Crystal Stone**	*Moses and Zipporah Attend a Roller Derby Game*
66	**Matt Robinson**	*Beer League*
68	**Sarah Key**	*A Mother's Ode to the Zamboni*

SL OUTDOORS

70	**Amy Jenkins**	*Shooting a Deer*
74	**Caroline Collins**	*Inheritance*

SL MISCELLANEOUS

76	**Kate Wright**	*Everyone's Portrait as Aaron Rodgers*
		Gymnasts' Salute
78	**Randy Steinberg**	*Playing the Masters*

SL BASEBALL

83	**Jeffrey Alfier**	*Song for a Practice Field*
84	**J.D. Scrimgeour**	*Portrait of the Poet as a Young Fan*
90	**Alinda Dickinson Wasner**	*RBIs*
92	**Daniel Southwell**	*The Soul of a Tigers' Fan*
96	**Bill Gruber**	*Jocks, Herbs, the '36 Yankees, Tea with Harold Bloom*
108	**Jerry Judge**	*Frank Robinson, 1956*

L

WHO'S ON FIRST

Sin and Baseball

—

William Loizeaux

My father was raised a Christian Brethren, my mother a Presbyterian, and while I was growing up, I was dimly aware that they'd worked out a deal. On Sunday mornings, my mother, in her pearls, heels and modestly stylish dresses, would take my two younger sisters and me to the Presbyterian Church in my hometown of Basking Ridge, New Jersey. There we'd attend Sunday school, and when we reached seven or eight years old, we'd sometimes join her in her favorite pew right up near the pulpit, where she'd belt out the hymns like Maria Callas. Then, after returning to our ranch-style house with my mother's yellow calico curtains in the kitchen windows, and after she, still humming the hymns, had grabbed her knitting, my father would finish shining his shoes, put on his brown, flecked tweed coat (whatever the weather), and we'd all squeeze into our rattly 1959 Ford Ranchwagon. A half hour later, at 915 Grant Avenue in Plainfield, my father's aging mother, fresh from the Christian Brethren Front Street Meeting, would be waiting for us, tapping her cane in the doorway of the old house where she'd brought up her family and lived for 50 years.

Here we entered a different world. Dark green drapes. Dark moldings. Dark rugs. Everywhere a faint mothball smell. All was still. All was quiet, except for the slow ticking of the grandfather clock in the front hallway, a clock about the size of a coffin. Time and death were always on my grandmother's mind. As was sin. That word on her lips above her whiskery chin carried a heavy weight. "The wages of sin is death. John 6:23," she'd remind my sisters and me. "Sin is lawlessness. John 3:14." "Sin is breaking the Law of God, especially The Ten Commandments."

Though I might have bent a few of them, at the age of eight in the winter of early-1961, I was pretty sure that I hadn't really broken those commandments. I didn't have any small-g gods above the big-G God in the sky. I didn't worship any statues, including those of the Virgin Mary, as did the Anderson boys next door. I didn't take the Lord's name in vain. I more or less honored my mother and father. I hadn't murdered anyone. I hadn't stolen anything of significance. I hadn't deceived my neighbors. Nor did I covet their servants, oxen, or donkeys, none of which I'd seen in our subdivision. As far as adultery goes, I had no idea what that meant. I wasn't an adult, so I thought I was in the clear on that one.

The stickiest wicket was "Keeping the Sabbath" — and I'm talking here about Sunday. For Presbyterians I knew, the Sabbath meant going to Sunday school or to the 9 or 11 a.m. service. It meant singing the hymns, sitting through the sermon and scripture readings, reciting the Lord's Prayer, putting change in the brass offering plate, and shaking Reverend Felmeth's hand on your way out the big double doors. That done, most Presbyterian kids could run around the neighborhood all afternoon and, depending on the season, swim in the Dickinsons' pool or skate on the Cortelyous' pond. On our way to Plainfield, I'd also see adults that I'd just seen at church whacking tennis balls on the Oak Street courts or golf balls at the Pennbrook Country Club. For Presbyterians, the Sabbath was a morning affair.

Not so for Christian Brethren. In my grandmother's house, the Sabbath was "kept holy" all day, a day for "rest and spiritual rejuvenation," and by keeping it, she told us, we'd ensure our eternal rest in God's kingdom. So no Parcheesi or Monopoly. No music. No TV. No radio. I now believe that

But not a one of all those biblical sinners or saints — not even Jesus — was tempted with such fruits as I was: Mel Allen, Phil Rizzuto, or that sweet voice of Red Barber calling Sunday Yankees games.

my grandmother loved us in her peculiar and demanding way, which was the way she loved her own children and the way she was loved by her parents and grandparents. It's also true that she served us delicious home-made caramel custard after our soup and grilled-cheese sandwich. But then she'd ask us all to file into her olive-green carpeted living room with those thick drapes, the gray sofa, and those bulky wingback chairs with doilies, like cobwebs, on their arms. In one of those chairs my father would sit with one leg crossed over the other, so you could see a half inch of his narrow white calf between his sock and the cuff of his flannel pants. In the chair across from him, my grandmother would sit with her cane leaning against her compression stockings, and her bottle of smelling salts and little black book of the Gospels in the crease of her lap. As my sisters in their Sunday smocked dresses and I in my Sunday jacket squirmed and fidgeted on the sofa, and as my mother sat in another chair knitting in a kind of quiet fury, my father, a mild, soft-spoken businessman who honored his mother, would listen and nod while my grandmother read from that little black book. Often a sad verse might remind her of her arthritis, of her "inside troubles," and — unscrewing the top of her smelling salts — of all our relatives in the family plot in Hillside Cemetery, "bless their souls."

I'm afraid that little of this felt very restful or rejuvenating to me — and not only because I was uneasy with or uninterested in the subject matter, but because I'd become very interested in another matter that would complicate the Sabbath. On a sunny Saturday in the summer of 1960, my maternal grandfather, a silver-haired Presbyterian in a straw hat and with two tickets sprouting from the breast pocket of his sport coat, had picked me up in Basking Ridge and driven me the forty or so miles, across the George Washington Bridge, to a Yankee game in the Bronx. It was an altogether innocent act of generosity and family fellowship, but unbeknownst to him or me, it started me down the darkening path toward perdition.

If you Google my last name and scroll down a few screens, you'll come upon the "Loizeaux Brothers," a small publishing house founded as the Bible Truth Depot by Paul and Timothy Loizeaux in the late 1800's. Between then and now, ownership of the publishing house passed from generation to generation within a branch of my family that I've never known though my grandmother did. By 1961, the Loizeaux Brothers had published 53 volumes of evangelical Christian Brethren literature, mostly biblical commentaries, extended meditations and sermons, all of which shared the Brethren tenets: the Bible is the sole authority in regard to matters of doctrine and practice; the consequence of sin is eternal death in hell, but salvation is available through repentance and faith in Jesus Christ, who will return as the messiah after "the rapture," in which all Christian believers will join him in eternity. H. A. Ironside, affectionately known among Brethren as the "Archbishop of Fundamentalism," wrote 41 of those volumes before his death in 1951. Many of his books and essays into which I've poked my nose have a cautionary, prophetic, and millennialist flavor, to say nothing of a certain moral stringency about them: *Holiness, the True and False, Death and Afterward,* and *Unless You Repent.* Other titles by other authors include *The End of this Present World, The Messianic Psalms, Heresies Exposed,* and a favorite topic that has nothing to do with your 401(k): *Eternal Security.*

I mention this because many, if not all, of these volumes, along with the framed photos of my paternal grandfather and others residing in Hillside

Cemetery, surrounded us on the shelves in my grandmother's living room. When it came to sin, holiness, and the disposition of your soul, the Loizeaux Brothers didn't fool around. This was serious business, a family business with the sort of stock-in-trade that often lit my eight-year-old imagination. In a flash, sin could ruin my life and afterlife. It would bore into me. It would cling to me. It would split me. It would engulf me. It didn't just mean I'd made a mistake. It wasn't something I could brush off with a few Hail Marys at the end of Confession, like the Anderson boys could do. Sin meant I'd die and, without any clothes on, be thrown into the lake of fire, where I'd swim in red-hot lava, and all I'd hear would be screams and grinding teeth, and everything would be smoky and orange and yellow and burning forever and ever… Unless I put my soul in the hands of the Lord, and really and truly repented. And then, by the grace of God, I might be saved.

So when my maternal grandfather had taken me to Yankee Stadium on that Saturday in the summer of 1960, I wasn't sinning, but I can see with all the clarity of retrospect that this was the thin edge of the wedge. The game was glorious, though I don't remember the score, who won, or even who was playing against the Yankees that day. We sat five rows behind the first base dugout, where we could watch — and hear! — the Yankee players as they trotted off and onto the field. Even now I can see every one of them fanned out in the sun and that scalloped shadow of the upper deck: Bob Turley on the mound, Eli Howard behind the plate; "Moose" Skowron, Richardson, Kubek, and Boyer around the infield; Maris in right, Mantle in center, Hecter Lopez way out there in left. We booed and cheered, my grandfather and I. We ate over-buttered popcorn. We drank soda, and with every batter, he scribbled on his scorecard hieroglyphics that he explained to me. I was a short, thin kid with a limp, but from that day until the end of his days, he would call me "Mantle," the incredibly swift, strong home run hitter, square-jawed and broad-shouldered, the hero of the team. And from then on I was in love — there is no other word for it — with him and with the Yankees. He and I wrote letters back and forth, and it was clear that, as a Presbyterian, he had no problem with listening to or even attending Sunday afternoon games. "Dear Mantle," his letters always began. "Did you hear about the game on Sunday?"

Well, I'd heard *about* it.

"Did you hear about the game on Friday night?"

Of course! I'd heard every minute! On weekdays and evenings that summer, I listened to Mel Allen, Phil Rizzuto, and Red Barber call the games on my parents' countertop Philco plugged into the socket between our stove and the sink. On Saturday afternoons, I watched the game on our living room TV, while my father read *The Plainfield Courier News* and my mother, ironing in the kitchen with the Philco at full blast, sang her heart out, tears and all, with the Metropolitan Opera. I learned how to read box scores. On lined yellow pads, I kept track of batting and earned run averages. I knew the line-up. I knew the pitching rotation. As the summer ended, I followed the pennant race with those pesky Orioles, and of course I kept writing back and forth with my grandfather. "Dear Mantle," he wrote on September 25th, "Congratulations! We clinched the pennant!" It was always "*we*," the first person plural, as if we'd helped make it happen by watching, keeping track, and listening.

Then at exactly 3:35 p.m. on Thursday, October 13, 1960, while I had my ear glued to the Philco after I'd raced home from school to catch the last inning of the seventh and deciding game of the World Series, the unthinkable happened. Heroically, the Yankees had tied the score in the top on the ninth, but in the bottom of that inning, on an 1-0 pitch from Yankee pitcher Ralph Terry, Bill Mazeroski — a second baseman, for goodness sake — hit a home run over the left field wall in Forbes Field to give the Pittsburgh Pirates a 10-9 win. And that was it. It was over. I couldn't believe my ears. I couldn't listen to the post-game recap. I wept for hours. I couldn't speak. I couldn't play outside with my friends. My mother let me stay home from school the next day. For a time, the world went dark and dead. Worst of all, I was partly to blame. If I'd had a hand in all those victories that season, wasn't I in some way responsible for *this*? Even my grandfather's cheery "We'll get them next year!" meant nothing to me.

I have no memories of the rest of that fall, though I understand the world still turned. From chronicles of the time, I know that the Yankees fired their beloved long-time manager, Casey Stengel, and Kennedy was elected President. It's only when I think of Christmas that year that my memory gets vivid and vibrant again. That morning, as we were gathered around the tree in our slippers and pajamas, I unwrapped a white, button-down shirt from my father, and from my mother, an AM transistor radio.

By late 1960, transistor radios (radios using tiny transistors rather than bulky vacuum tubes as their active electronic components) had only been on the market for a few years and had been too expensive for most middle-class families. Slowly, the prices were coming down, but the $26.95 (about $220 today) that my mother shelled out for that brand new radio must have busted her annual "Christmas Fund" saved up from her paychecks for teaching middle school math. The radio was a pocket-size Lafayette, and came with a brown leather case. On the outside of the case, beneath a fan-shaped opening that let you see the station numbers on the radio, "Lafayette" was inscribed in fancy, French-looking script. Beneath that was a perfect grid of BB-sized holes that let you hear the sound inside. But it wasn't until you unsnapped the two fasteners on the back of the case, pulled the carrying strap forward, and slid out the radio itself that you beheld, right there in your palm, the wonder of it all.

I have a number of friends my age who still don't understand the talismanic power of iPhones, and especially that power in the hands of kids. They don't understand how kids can't walk or sit or practically breathe without their fingers curled around a piece of plastic.

I do. Because all those years ago, I couldn't walk or sit or practically breathe without my own fingers around my Lafayette, model FS-91 "Mighty 9" nine-transistor radio. Though I haven't held it for almost sixty years, I still know that radio in the way that I know my wallet in the pocket of my pants. According to an August 29, 1960 ad in Billboard Magazine, the radio measured 4.5 inches high, 3.0 inches wide, 1.25 inches deep, and weighed 9 ounces. Like the iPhone, it was rounded at every corner, but unlike the iPhone's harsh, straight sides, the Mighty 9 had the gracefully bowed sides of a canoe or a rowboat, like skin stretched smooth over ribs. On the top half of its face, above the silver grill protecting the speaker, stood a gold crown, fanning out as it rose. In the middle of the crown a tiny needle pointed to your favorite station, which you tuned in by adjusting the dial set deeply into the left side, like a coin in a slot. On the other side, also more felt than seen, was the dial to adjust the volume and turn the radio on and off. And when you did turn it on, it responded *immediately*, as the tiny capacitors, transistors, and transformers went into action. Moreover, it gave off a subtle smell, a bouquet with hints of ozone, plastic, and solder flux that I can best describe as *intimate*. Everything about that radio was intimate, and I sensed it all on that Christmas morning. The way it fit into my hand. The feel of those tiny teeth on the dials. That slight resistance, the soft giving way and that satisfying *click* as I turned it on. The way it would speak, sing, or seemed to breathe directly into my ear. The way, without its case, it slid into my pocket. The way I could take it into my room and still it spoke to me. The way it revealed its insides — those mysterious little cylinders, squares, and squiggles of colored wire — when I opened its back to put in the batteries.

Roughly four to five million transistor radios were sold by the end of 1960, so my experience was hardly unique. For the rest of that winter, my radio was more or less attached to me whenever I was at home, and I rarely listened to the kitchen Philco. This was right when Top-40 AM radio was becoming popular, and it didn't take long for me to tune in to WABC Musicradio 77 from New York City. I listened to DJs Jack Carney and Chuck Donovan, and when I was allowed to stay up late on Friday nights, I'd hear Scott "Scottso" Muni spinning hits like "Will You Love Me Tomorrow," "Shop Around," "Good Time Baby," and "I'm in the Mood for Love," all of which had an obscure and uncomfortable allure.

In April, the baseball season started again, and I was desperate to heal the heartache of the last World Series. How would the Yankees play without Casey Stengel? Could they pull themselves back together? After school, I listened to the remainders of games, and on Saturdays I heard every inning or watched on WPIX TV, but on Sunday afternoons at my grandmother's house, I was still baseball-deprived.

Then sometime in mid-April, it came to me like a whisper that was quieter but more powerful and persistent than the allure of those top-40 hits: *What if?... What if I just happen to have my radio in my pocket when we go to Grandmother's house? And what if, when we're there, I figure out how to listen to games without anyone hearing...or seeing...or knowing?*

As my grandmother reminded us and would have been happy to tell you, the Bible is full of people who succumb to temptation, who sin and literally catch hell for it, while others who "refuse Satan" move confidently along the path to salvation. Right off the bat, there were Adam and Eve who were tossed out of Eden. There was David, who — though I couldn't grasp how this was a sin — "lay with" the bathing beauty Bathsheba, and for it their son died by the hand of the Lord. Perhaps even worse was the fate of Achan, who was caught stealing. "All of Israel stoned him to death!" my grandmother said.

On the brighter side, there were Abraham and Elijah, who wouldn't take money or riches for anything. There was Joseph, who wouldn't "lay with" Potiphar's wife. And of course there was Jesus in the wilderness.

Hearing the Bible stories that my grandmother read to us, I was frightened by the examples of those who sinned and awed by those who turned their backs on temptation. But not a one of all those biblical sinners or saints — not even Jesus — was tempted with such fruits as I was: Mel Allen, Phil Rizzuto, or that sweet voice of Red Barber calling Sunday Yankees games.

So on a Sunday in late April of 1961, when my mother, sisters and I were home from the Presbyterian Church, I slid my radio into the inside pocket of my jacket, and off we all went to Plainfield. Now and then as we travelled, I lightly touched that pocket in the nervous and reassuring way that Catholic girls touched their rosary beads. I was still touching it as we went into my grandmother's house and after lunch when, listening to her in the living room, an idea gradually dawned. As those books on my grandmother's shelves would have warned, this is how sin works. It worms into your tiniest crevices, grows imperceptibly, overtakes you, then cracks you open.

I slumped on the sofa and grimaced as in pain.

"What's wrong?" my grandmother asked, frowning and looking up from her little black book.

"Oh, nothing..."

Then before my grandmother got going again, my mother stopped her knitting and studied my face. "What is it?"

I shrugged my shoulders but grimaced again.

"You aren't going to get sick, are you?" my father said, suddenly energized.

"Oh, for heaven's sake!" my grandmother said.

"He's going to throw up!" my sisters cried, bolting up from the sofa.

"No, I don't think so," my mother said calmly. She set her knitting aside, came over and put the back of her wrist against my forehead. "I think you're okay, but maybe you should go upstairs and take a rest."

This sounded reasonable to everyone. So, stricken, I dragged myself out of the living room and climbed the stairs to the second floor guest bedroom.

It was another dark, green room, more the color of pine trees than olives, though the darkness there didn't trouble me. In fact, I darkened it even more by closing the door and pulling the window blind down to the sill. In the remaining light, I could make out the bureau, and in one corner a cushy armchair with an ottoman in front of it, a comfortable enough place to rest, but what I really needed was the bed. I pulled back the spread. I kicked off my shoes. I slid the Mighty 9 out of my jacket pocket… And suddenly I *was* feeling sick, like when you're squished in the back seat of a 1959 Ranchwagon and you go over that bump on Long Hill Road, and for a time everything is sweaty and queasy.

When I turn it on, how far will the sound of my radio go? Will they hear it downstairs? And what if I get caught — caught breaking the Sabbath? What about the lake of fire?

Then, slowly settling my stomach, there came a soft, smooth, increasingly precipitous sliding feeling that I couldn't and didn't want to stop.

I can do this. I can get away with it.

I held the radio in the cup of my hands. I clicked it on. With the volume low, I slipped it under the pillow to muffle the sound. Getting on the bed, I lay my head on the pillow, my ear right over the radio, and with a keen and guilty pleasure that seemed all mine, I closed my eyes. Listening to every word, I drifted away from that room, that house with those books and those photos on the shelves, and my grandmother reading downstairs… I smelled the popcorn and tasted the soda. I heard the crowd. I saw the green field, the brown warning track, the smudgy chalk-lined batter's boxes, the shadow of the upper deck, the player's sleeves flapping in the breeze. I saw Clete Boyer stab a grounder down the line. I watched my grandfather mark his scorecard. I saw Mantle at the plate, his front shoulder drawing back like a catapult, his front leg extending, his rear one bending, and then his hips and shoulders unwinding as with an explosion, and his bat miss the ball or absolutely crush it…

During the middle innings of the game that afternoon, there was a tap on the door. The knob turned slowly, and in the shaft of light that came in the room, I saw in silhouette my mother's head with her thin neck and wavy hair.

"How are things going?"

"Better," I said. "Pretty good,"

She cocked her head as if she'd heard something that made her curious, but she didn't come in the room. Then she whispered, "Are we winning?"

Though it was hard to believe what I'd just heard, I lifted my head and nodded.

"Well, let's keep it that way," she said.

The shaft of light narrowed as she closed the door.

This breaking the Sabbath went on for the rest of that summer and early fall. While it was clear that I was often sick on Sunday afternoons, no one seemed to notice that my headaches or stomach aches corresponded exactly with the starting times of Yankee games: 1 p.m. for double-headers, 2 p.m. for single games, and some away games would start a few hours later.

"What's *wrong* with him?" I'd hear my grandmother say as I climbed the stairs.

"Yeah?!" one of my sisters would ask.

"Growing pains," my mother explained, her needles clicking steadily. "Leave him be."

If you know anything about baseball, you'll probably know something about the 1961 season. That was when the Yankees won 109 games and lost 53, including 23 wins and only 11 losses on Sundays. That was the season when Yankee pitcher Whitey Ford won 25 games and didn't lose one on a Sunday. Most memorably, it was the season when Mickey Mantle and Roger Maris chased Babe Ruth's record of 60 home runs. As it happened, Mantle hit a home run on the Yankee's first Sunday game of that year. On the last, October 1st, Maris hit his record-breaking 61st — and I heard it, Phil Rizzuto making the call: "A fastball… Hit deep to right!.. Way back there!! Hol-y Cow!!"

Never has the Sabbath been so deliciously violated, so gloriously unholy, so un-kept. My grandmother was right. The Loizeaux Brothers were right. Given a toehold, sin engulfed me. It cleaved me. And cloven I became what I've been ever since — and maybe what, to some degree, we all are: the kid who went to church on Sunday mornings and the kid who lay with his Lafayette Mighty 9 in that darkened guest room on those Sunday afternoons, when I sinned with all my heart and soul.

Today my father and grandmother are buried a few yards apart in the family plot in Hillside Cemetery, a five-minute drive from the old house in Plainfield. My mother, now ninety-four, lives in Atlanta, near my youngest sister, and she has left instructions in no uncertain terms that her ashes be buried in the Presbyterian churchyard in Basking Ridge. As for her father, my baseball-loving grandfather, he lies with his Presbyterian forbears in a cemetery in Bayonne, New Jersey, about 20 miles down the Hudson from Yankee Stadium.

And me? I'm quite alive, sitting here at my desk, trying to figure out what might become of the souls of my grandfather, myself, and other sinful Sabbath baseball fans. Of course, I could settle the issue by arguing that there is no such thing as a soul. Or I could argue that, if there is and its final destination depends on one's earthly behavior and faith, keeping the Sabbath might not be as imperative as other commandments, and violating it might not deserve an afterlife in the flames, especially if, like Presbyterians, you've only violated half of it.

But, putting aside the direct approach to these weighty questions for the moment, I note that baseball itself flirts with notions of sin and salvation and may even have some modest suggestions for our consideration.

According to scholars, the word sin derives from the Greek ἁμαρτία or *hamartia*, which can mean "failing to hit the target" or "missing the mark" and first applied to spear throwing or archery. You sinned when you missed the mark. For baseball fans, this may ring a bell. When a pitcher fails to hit the target, or the catcher's mitt, when he throws too many curves in the dirt, high fastballs, or hits a batter, he is said to be missing the mark. And if he misses the mark with a man on base who advances to another base, he is charged with a wild pitch, or a WP in the box score. In theological terms, we might say he has sinned. He has succumbed to his — and our — original, inherited wildness and chaos that resulted from Adam's Fall. In baseball terms, he has "lost his stuff," "lost his command," or "lost control." And if repeatedly, game after game, a big league pitcher misses the mark, he'll be damned, sent down to the minors, where he'll sit on sweltering busses between Altoona and Trenton and play on dusty fields before 1,539 customers, most of whom are in the bleachers because it's Ten Cent Beer Night or Clunker Car Night. These are the wages of sin.

Yet there can be another result of sin in baseball, even on that dusty field in Altoona, when you've sinned egregiously, when your team that once had a big lead is ahead by a run in the bottom of the eighth, and now you've walked two straight batters and the bases are loaded with only one out, and your arm feels like meat in a casing, and you know exactly where you're going if you don't get out of this: down to a team like the Lansing Lugnuts or the Batavia Muckdogs, down to the very bottom of hell, to single-A ball.

Even then it can happen. It often does. Along with your manager, another guy a little younger than you and in the same uniform you're wearing, joins you on the mound and takes the ball which you've just handed to the manager before you leave the game. He's a lanky, regular-looking guy whose arm is fresh and who can throw a fastball in the mid-90s and a knee-buckling curve on the outside corner that the next batter will hit on the ground to short, an easy 6-4-3 double play that will end the inning and get you off the hook.

Then the next day you'll read it in the Scriptures, right there near the bottom of the box score. Beside your name is a W, which means you won the game, and beside the name of your relief pitcher, it says SV, short for Save.

I don't know what's happened to my grandfather's soul, or what will happen to mine and to that of other Sabbath sinners. How can anyone know that sort of thing? What I do know is that in baseball you are not saved if you pitch a complete game, a complete no-hitter, or even a perfect game. You are not saved by piety. You are not saved by perfection. In baseball, as in many religions and sects, you must sin to be saved. But importantly, you need not repent. Nor does salvation come by the grace of God, nor by faith in anyone or anything larger, more holy or righteous than you, but instead by the work of that lanky, regular-looking guy, who likely has committed sins as interesting as yours, who took your place, did his job, and after the game took a shower, got dressed in his T-shirt and jeans, and had a few beers with you down at the Billy Goat. In baseball, sin, within limits, is almost inevitable, an expected and acceptable part of the game. You will do it. You will lose your stuff and miss the mark. Then you will be relieved — and if all goes well, saved. You will walk from the mound and into the dugout, from the surface of the earth to a place dug out of it. And if the guys on your team who remain on the field can pitch, catch, and do what they're supposed to do, there's a pretty good chance that your soul, if you have one, will be okay.

———

Bill Loizeaux, raised in New Jersey, has always been a Yankee fan. Now, with some unease, he lives in Boston, in the dark shadow of Fenway Park. He has published essays, stories and award-winning nonfiction and fiction books for children and adults. His memoir *Anna: A Daughter's Life* was a *New York Times* Notable Book. His children's novel *Wings* was the winner of the 2006 Henry Bergh Children's Award in Fiction. His adult novel, *The Tumble Inn*, was the grand prize winner at the 2015 New York Book Festival. Another children's novel is forthcoming in April, 2021. Meanwhile, he has been a road department worker, a greenskeeper's assistant, a house painter, and Writer-in-Residence at a couple of universities. But what would he really like? To have played centerfield — if only for a day — on a sunny Sunday afternoon in Yankee Stadium. Learn more at WilliamLoizeaux.com.

L

How to Repair a Bicycle

—

Michael Kula

(handwritten annotation: conversational)

First, you will need a bicycle, of course. No doubt you've had others before. That Kmart mountain bike you bought with good intentions for commuting, but never rode. That gray and pink Cannondale from the 1980s you borrowed from your big brother to try your hand at triathlons. But those are both long gone by now, left behind or sold during one of your cross-country moves.

But don't worry. Finding a bike will be the easy part. Especially if it's summer and that big brother of yours — Jeff — has stage four lung cancer. At your house, half of the continent away from his, you will have what seems like endless idle time. So drive around on weekends, look for garage sales. You will find one. The first: 40 bucks at a yard sale a block from your house.

So, take it home. Put it in your basement. Pull out tools — inappropriate ones, ones you use for home renovation and plumbing — and start removing the parts. You won't know the proper names for things yet. Not derailleur, not bottom bracket, not freewheel. Right now, they are all just random parts, and so you will break some, scratch others, and eventually you will end up with a bare frame and an accompanying pile of metal that makes no sense. It will remind you of the time you taught yourself woodworking, making the highchair for your newborn son. All that wasted lumber piled on the floor from your mistakes. No, there will be no putting this bike back together.

So buy another bike. Craigslist this time. A shiny Motobecane from the 1970s for $30. Do all the same things again, with all the same high ambitions. You will fail again, but just stick the parts with the others in the corner of the room where your furnace is, and buy another bike. Do the same with it. Repeat as necessary, until your children start calling that room in your basement "the bike room."

By the end of summer, the chemo the doctor had told your brother would work like "magic" will stop being magic at all, and the bikes will come even more quickly then. Your wife will roll her eyes at the sight of each one you wheel through the kitchen, and she'll tell you often that you need help.

Downstairs, you'll look at the buckets of parts you've amassed, the naked frames shivering in the corner, and you'll agree, though not in the way she had intended. Yes, you think. You do need help. You were supposed to be repairing things.

So, go get help, even if it's not the kind your wife meant. Buy proper bike tools; read thick maintenance manuals; post questions in bicycle chatrooms; watch hours of YouTube tutorials once the house falls asleep. You might, by then, actually succeed in putting a bike back together. Fixing it. And it will feel good to watch that college girl ride away from your house on that Schwinn you sold her for half as much as it was worth. This will feel good. Great even.

But this feeling will be short lived. With the start of autumn your brother will switch to hospice care, and you will say fuck all those bikes. Fuck that pile of garbage you made downstairs. You would back over it with your car if you could. And so you don't touch another bike for more than a month. Not until you are back in Nashville with your family in October, where you will find yourself taking apart Jeff's bicycle two days before his funeral. The Cannondale he rode with his Italian friend Andrea on weekends. The bike he told you that he wanted you to have last time you saw him. Take it apart in your parent's living room as though it's made of glass, wrapping each part twice before packing it in the box to ship back to your home. In the middle of this, you will realize that all those hours of breaking down bikes in your basement had at least been good for something.

Back home, don't open that box for a while. Try to ignore it, even though it's impossible to miss leaning there against the fireplace in the back of your living room and go back to buying bikes. They are even cheaper now, easier to find with the end of riding season approaching. They are like rabbits in your basement, you think. With each new one you bring home, you'll watch your children lose any amusement they once had at seeing dad work on his bikes. And your wife will tell you once more that you need help. And, again, you will agree with her; but, again, you'll mean it in your own way.

And so, after that, go dig that one bike out of the rubble downstairs. The 1986 Raleigh Alyeska you bought back in August, your "holy grail" bike, as the people in the chatrooms might call it. It's burgundy and bordeaux, according to its original catalog description, and you know it will make a beautiful bike. A keeper. Until now you've been afraid to touch it, afraid you'll mess it up, and so go get the help you need at the community bike shop in town. Spend three rainy weekends there being tutored by a kid named Travis, who has a mohawk and smells like a mix of axel grease and pot. From him, you'll learn how to take it apart properly. And, how to put it back together. The *right* way. At last, you will know how to repair a bicycle.

When you finish, that Raleigh will be as good as new. Better than new, actually, complete with a $140 Brooks saddle and a $90 roll of handle bar tape — real leather — which each cost more than double what you paid for the bike itself. Take that bike home and leave it in the living room like a trophy, leaning against that still unopened box with Jeff's bike. And just like that, Christmas will pass, the rainy season will begin to slow — though the days won't seem any less dark — and the Raleigh will still sit there, untouched. Every day when you see it after work, you'll wish you could show it to your brother. Like how, as a kid, you would call him to tell him about some accomplishment you had. You'll wish, too, that you could invite him out that coming summer for a ride in the mountains. But of course, you can't. And that's when it will hit you. Maybe all of this isn't about *how* to repair a bicycle, but rather *why* repair a bicycle. They're meant for riding, after all.

And so, the next rain-free day you get, change into those tight shorts you own — tighter than you recall now after an idle winter — and wheel that bike out onto your porch. Your wife will see this and look at you with surprise, but thankfully not say a word before you leave. In the street in front of your house, swing your leg over the top bar, hop on the stiff saddle, and coast down the hill. At first, it will feel like you are flying, like the first time you rode a bike, as best you can recall, and it will be easy to keep going, eventually reaching the big park at the edge of your city. Once you're there, don't turn around for home — not yet — even though you know tomorrow your legs will be sore from this. Instead, keep going, do a five-mile loop through the massive fir trees.

There, beneath them, you will feel small. And alone. And cold in those growing shadows of the coming sunset. But you will feel proud, too. Proud that you saved that bike, saved it from the shed at that estate sale where it was going to rust away if you hadn't bought it. Then, you will think about your brother, of course, and you will do your best to keep riding a little farther before turning for home, even as the wind stings your face.

—

Michael Kula is a graduate of the MFA program in Creative Writing at Emerson College, and he is associate professor of writing studies at the University of Washington, Tacoma. His work has previously appeared in numerous literary journals, both online and in print, and his novel *The Good Doctor* was published in 2017 by Urban Farmhouse Press. He is currently completing his second book, a nonfiction account of the life and travels of a Polish journalist who bicycled across Africa in the 1930s. He lives in Tacoma with his wife and two children, and when he isn't writing or teaching, you might find him biking somewhere in the mountainous Pacific Northwest or else planning for his next bike tour with friends.

OUR ALL-AMERICANS

Since our Chicago founding in 1995, we've been lucky enough to field 22 writers (a virtual football team) whose *Sport Literate* essays earned notable nods in two "Best American" anthologies. Two more were republished in *Best American Sports Writing*.

Notable Essays in *The Best American Sports Writing*:

1. Frank Soos, "Obituary with Bamboo Fly Rod," 1997
2. Mark Wukas, "Running with Ghosts," 1998
3. Frank Soos, "On His Slowness," 1999
4. Molly Moynahan, "Don't Walk," 2000
5. Jay Lesandrini, "Waiting on Deck," 2010
6. Frank Soos, "Another Kind of Loneliness," 2013
7. Dave Essinger, "Hallucinating in Suburbia: John Cheever, Buddha, and the Unabomber on the Urban Ultramarathon," 2014
8. Alessandra Nolan, "Channeling Mr. Jordan," 2016
9. Laura Legge, "The Responsible Player," 2017
10. Liz Prato, "Flights of Two," 2018

Notable Essays in *The Best American Essays*:

1. Michael Steinberg, "Elegy for Ebbets," 2002
2. William Huhn, "The Triple Crown," 2004
3. Robert Parker, "The Running of the Bull," 2006
4. Benedict Giamo, "Played Out," 2009
5. Peter Stine, "Detroit Marathon," 2010
6. Cinthia Ritchie, "Running," 2012
7. Katie Cortese, "Winning Like a Girl," 2014
8. Gayle Brandeis, "IceTown," 2016
9. Rachel Luria, "The Rush Gives Warmth Enough," 2016
10. Phillip A. Snyder, "Rental Horses," 2016
11. Michael J. Hess, "On the Morning After the Crash," 2017
12. Liz Prato, "Flights of Two," 2018

Republished Essays In *The Best American Sports Writing*:

- Mark Pearson, "The Short History of an Ear," 2010
- Cinthia Ritchie, "Running," 2012

Our *Best American Essays* Notable Special Issues:

- 2004 "Father's Issue"
- 2006 "Retrospective Reflections"
- 2009 "Our Football Best"

POETRY

Helmet

—

Laura Madeline Wiseman

No red in the pre-dawn skyline, no front pushing
in the distance, no incessant seams to jar clear
the night terrors. Holey styrofoam is all there is

to replace what cracked in that car-bicycle collision,
that shock that made this state a strange,
dangerous journey — bruised, bone-ached,

shaken — to teach how much is held, how tenuous
a hold. Could another helmet, with its straps dangling
against the throat, be security? Could any Nutcase

or Bell, any pattern protect what needs to be cradled?
Could a new talisman like the stars and stripes on a crown
hold you — one of ten states down, nine to go,

almost like fingers that cup a furry not-quite roadkill,
or like a pitcher's glove around what you could throw
if this were a field, or like a waffle fry, that heat

and salt, that means a friend just bought you dinner?
Could that cross-country spirit soften the possible falls,
keep you together, catches locked, with maximum airflow?

You go on — what choice is there, if this is it? To be a visible dot
moving along the road, you align the visor to block the sun.
You put us on like any pioneer bonnet, any stovepipe hat

of hardscrabble past. Who says America is broken or small?
Who says you can't be covered by it as you cover it,
shore to shore by bicycle, just to prove it's possible?

Trail Cyclers Inn at Al's Place

—

Laura Madeline Wiseman

Al arrives after first or second supper
to be the good bunkbed night, two dollar
laundry washes, and free outlets everywhere
to charge each flickering device,

to be the good bug-free morning,
showered, and hot breakfasted. *Al's Fantastic*
social sites rate this cyclist hostel,
and Al, gawd, it's great you exist.

It's the twentieth full day of the trail
and for days, it's been miles searching
to feel anything familiar — humidity,
sated hunger, a well-earned sleep.

If you were once a prison, Al,
now we're all free as the road calls
to finally understand privilege —
AC, kitchen, couches, indoor parking.

All night you protect us by a key code
and hold onto what's important —
bicycles, dreams, the map of tomorrow.
All along you were here, Al. Now we know.

Road Flare

—

Laura Madeline Wiseman

So maybe she's just a broken headband,
but one perfect pigtail remains and you've got it —
curl, hues of blonde-orange that brightens,
one magenta sparking strand that glints,
and a spring ready to jiggle to the edge
of Richmond. What head did she hold
with giggles on the Virginia Capital Trail?

Maybe that's all there will ever be — just that
one bit of fluff that catches the light
among the shadows, some piece missed
by the mowers who come back for the trash.
Or maybe this fluff is everywhere and other
cyclists like you, are remembering how it once felt
to have hair tucked behind the ears, bouncing
with the grade on the Colonial Parkway
and like kids — that fearless — reach for light.

These poems originally appeared in What a Bicycle Can Carry *(BlazeVOX books, 2018).*

—

Laura Madeline Wiseman teaches writing at the University of Nebraska-Lincoln. Her book Velocipede (Stephen F. Austin State University Press), is a 2016 Foreword INDIES Book of the Year Award Finalist for Sports. Her essays and poems on bicycles have appeared in *Sport Literate*, *Boneshaker Magazine*, *Adventure Cycling* blog, and elsewhere. Her latest book is *A Bicycle's Echo* (Red Dashboard, 2018), a collection of essays on cycling that includes the 41st New Millennium Writings Literary Awards for Nonfiction finalist essay "Finding the Gap on Dead Man's Run" and the *Pacifica Literary Review's* 2015 Creative Honorable Mention Nonfiction Award-winning essay "Seven Cities of Good." Learn more: lauramadelinewiseman.com

Support
PUT YOUR MONEY WHERE
YOUR PENNANT IS

Sport Literate donations begin at $66.
See page 5 for details.

L

ESSAY

Random Numbers from a Summer of Alaska Trail Running

—

Cinthia Ritchie

17: Number of bears you see out on the trails

It happens so quickly, so unexpectedly, the way danger always veers into your life. One moment you're running through birch and alder trees, mountains rising in the distance, your feet dodging rocks and tree roots. The next moment there's a rustle in the brush and a bear charges out onto the trail. There's no time to think or even feel fear. You back away. You do this slowly, the way you were taught. You back away, all the while noting your surroundings as if even now, in this moment of calm apprehension, a wiser, more instinctual self has taken over, calculating clues and escape routes, the best possible method of avoiding trouble.

But there's no need for such assessments, not this time. The bear pauses for an agonizing moment, both of you standing silent and still, and then quickly veers back into the brush. You wait for a minute, to make sure it's gone, and then begin running again. You imagine that it's chasing you, that loping stride of a bear, that terrifying gait much faster than yours. Your heart pounds and you pick up the pace. You don't slow down until you pass two people walking a dog miles up the trail.

"I just saw a bear," you want to tell them. But you don't. You hoard this to yourself, not so much out of fear as out of selfishness, and wonder. You want to keep this moment to yourself.

5: Number of times you bleed

You fall more often than you'd like. This is unavoidable. You are clumsy, and the trails are obstinate with roots and rocks and bad footing. You can't stop lifting your eyes to take in the view, the mountains spreading around you, the rocked ledges, the sky so near that once you raised your arms, sure you could touch a raven flying overhead. That's when you fell, during that small blink of inattention, your knee slamming a rock, your skin opening like a newly formed word. You picked yourself up, kept running, a trail of blood behind you. Even though it rained the next day, you still like to think of your blood painting the dirt, soaking in to the rocks, that years from now it will still be there, like those petroglyphs you've seen on Arizona cliffs: I was here, once.

73: Number of times you pee in the bushes

You do this so often that it becomes second nature, the way you step off to the side of the trail, pull down your shorts and let loose. The mountains rising in the background, the scrub spruce and alders casting their bored shadows. Sometimes, though not often, in fact it's very rare but sometimes someone passes by and catches you in the act. You nod, pull up your shorts, continue on your way. You feel no need to apologize; there's no sense of modesty out here, no buildings or semblance of man, nothing but wild country, and wind. Sometimes, when you finish, you pat the ground with loving familiarity. You imagine Native American women walking this same earth years ago as they followed the hunt or headed to fish camp. Often, and you feel shy to admit this, but often you feel as if you are marking this land you love so much, leaving a part of yourself behind, the way wolves mark their territory with the scent of their own urine. We are all, and you understand this more with each run, nothing but animals with wild and wicked hearts.

3: Number of times you puke

Your stomach has never been your strong point. Growing up, the country doctor you visited labeled you with a sensitive intestinal tract and you have fond memories lying on the couch in the afternoons while your sisters were at school, the afghan pulled up to your chest as you watched afternoon game shows on TV. You've since taught yourself to be tough, to be able to handle anything, to run with too little food or too much of the wrong food. You've eaten avocado sandwiches and hummus with crackers and even jerky tofu while on long runs, and for the most part your stomach cooperates. Except when it doesn't. Each time this happens, each time your stomach protests, that small ache that grows larger with each passing mile, acid swimming your throat until you are forced to stop, lean over and hurl it all back up again; each time this happens, you feel both punished and redeemed. You cover this vomit with sticks and leaves, you bury it like a dead thing, like a shame or secret you want no one to witness. Whenever you run past these sites, these graveyards of your weakness, these monuments to your inability to process food while hauling your tired ass up a mountain, you make an invisible sign of the cross, the way you used to in church. Running and religion, you understand, are merged so close together that you can never be sure where the praying leaves off and the suffering begins.

9: Number of eagles you see

You've always wanted to fly, that's the superpower you'd choose, if you had the chance. When you were younger you used to leap from the hayloft, arms flapping and that brief moment of flight, of your body airborne before it crashed into the scratchy mounds of hay. It's a moment you still long for, you still seek. Maybe that's why you feel such a kinship with the eagles, why you envy their long stretch of wings, their graceful flight. You know that this is the reason you run, not for the speed as for the motion, that sense of leaving your body, of not exactly flying but not exactly staying on the ground, either.

11: Number of times you pass no one the whole run

You run at odd times, in odd places, veering off on side trails, the less populated, the better. You like hills and mud, you like to sweat and grit your teeth. You like being out there in the woods and mountains alone, just you and the dog, the sound of your footsteps as comforting as a voice. Inevitably, you'll pass someone every few miles, a hiker or a biker or another runner, and you'll nod in solitary appreciation. What you cherish most are those runs when you find yourself truly alone, when you sink so deeply inside your head that you forget who you are and where you are, your breath steady and fast, the sky stretching out above you, on and on like the sound of your heartbeat. Once, last winter, you came upon a skier dying of a heart attack in the middle of the trail and you stopped, offered assistance that wasn't needed. Still, you didn't leave, couldn't leave. You stood there in that soft, blue twilight, the air cold, the snow hushed and secretive, you stood with your dog and sang in a soft and low voice, serenading this death, this passage. Your hands empty and cold: It was the only thing you had to offer, the only thing you knew to give.

26: Number of times you cry

You often cry while running, sometimes in pain, sometimes in loneliness, sometimes in unexpected happiness. The longer you run, the better the chances that you'll cry. It's one of the reasons you seek out distances, one of the reasons you'd rather run 20 miles than do just about anything else. You love the way the miles buff away your defenses, your pride and accomplishments falling away until you are left egoless, a formless and newly-born thing. You are no one, running through valleys and splashing through creeks. You are a woman of no age, no past, no urgencies or regrets, and at the same time you are every woman who has ever run or wanted to run or couldn't because she wasn't permitted. Your lungs expand, your breath sucks in the same air that millions of women before you breathed, women you will never meet or know; that no one will remember. Still, sometimes you can hear them, out there in that clean mountain air, the whisper of their voices, the sound of their laughter, and this makes you cry, tears streaming down your face as you run back and forth in time, running because you can, because you are lucky enough to have the body and privilege and opportunity to run, and you swear to never take this for granted, to never take it lightly, not the running so much as what it gives you, these moments of clarity, of your body moving through vast and open spaces. You cry because you know that one day this will end.

1: Number of lynx you see

Summer is almost over now, the silver twilight spreading across the land by nine o'clock, and already you're feeling nostalgic for the light and the warm air and all that will soon be lost. You're running up the Powerline Pass loop with a friend, everything quiet and lush, the air smelling damp from the rain. Trudging up that long and lonely hill, your breath gasping, your legs screaming for you to slow down. Right before you reach the crest that opens vast views across the valley, you notice a movement from the corner of your eye. You stop, startled. You're expecting a bear or a moose, but a lynx magically appears, padding towards you on its big, soft paws. It slows down but shows no fear, only a mild curiosity, as if wondering who you are and why you're out running so late at night, when other two-leggeds have abandoned the world to the animals, to the rightful wanderers of the trails and mountains. You stand silent, staring at one another. Its eyes so yellow they're almost green, and those funny sprouts of hair poking up from its ears. You slow down your breath, as if to make this moment last. Soon, too soon, it turns and walks off down the trail. Its paws make no sound. It doesn't look back. Probably, it's already forgotten that you were ever there.

Cinthia Ritchie is an Alaska writer, ultra-runner and three-time Pushcart Prize nominee. Find her work at *New York Times Magazine*, *Evening Street Review*, *Sport Literate*, *Rattle*, *Best American Sports Writing*, *Mary*, *Into the Void*, *Clementine Unbound*, *Deaf Poets Society*, *Forgotten Women* anthology, *Nasty Women* anthology, *Hunger Journal*, *Gyroscope Review*, *Bosque Literary Journal* and others. She's a 2013 *Best American Essay* notable mention, and her first novel *Dolls Behaving Badly* was published by Hachette Book Group.

POETRY

Surprising

—

Kara Thom

How the redundancy of a daily five-mile run
could end tragically. A block from home.

Neighbors depended on seeing you — looked for you,
especially, when it was ten below — but couldn't protect you.

What does consistency matter in the end?

You lived to say you played piano
every day, including the day you died.

Believing in routines, logs, details, except,
you couldn't remember to zip your own fly.

Ultimately good clean living was no match for the impact.

But this, she will never forget: Your granddaughter
fell asleep in your arms the last time you saw her.

And who knows what might have been beyond seventy-eight years.
A diagnosis? Memory loss? A sudden decline in health?

Or, the alternative we mourn? Warm winters in Florida, reigning
at shuffleboard. Cooking for your wife. Dying peacefully in your sleep.

No matter the surprise ending, consistency outlived you:
Your race number for the next 10K already assigned.

In Memory of John Miklethun

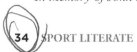

Kara Douglass Thom is a freelance writer and author of 10 books, including *Becoming an Ironman: First Encounters with the Ultimate Endurance Event* and the children's book series for the Go! Go! Sports Girls. Her poetry has appeared in the anthology, *Weaving the Terrain: 100-Word Southwestern Poems* and several online journals. She is the 2018 recipient of the Gaia Fenna Memorial Fellowship at Tofte Lake Center for Artists. She lives in Chaska, Minnesota, with her husband and four children, where she often finds inspiration for her work while running the trails near her home.

L

Five Running Shorts

—

Scott F. Parker

The Joy of Running qua Running

Recently I heard something in an old Alan Watts' lecture that made me question the way we talk about running. It seems to me that more often than not we talk about it in the way we talk about everything else — as another duty to be squeezed into our already busy and productive lives. You know the attitude: whether it's waking up early to get in three miles before work or running during the lunch break or stopping off at the gym to hit the treadmill on the way home, we must keep up with our responsibility to stay in shape (or, more dire, to get in shape). Running is one more thing we *have to* do. It's one more thing that's *good for us.*

But what could be more absurd than running because it's good for us? We're all dying all the time. Any decade now, each of us will be gone.

"True," these Good for Yous say, "but don't you know if you run you'll get an extra part of a decade added on at the end?"

I can't help but recall the old Woody Allen joke: *this food is terrible — and such small portions.* Who wants to do something they don't want to do in order to have more time in which to do things they don't want to do?

If running is good for us it's good in the way that breathing air and drinking water are good for us. No one ever said, "I've thought about it and I've decided to breathe some air." Or: "I reviewed the data and it would be wise for me to drink this water." No. We drink water because we're thirsty. We breathe air because as soon as we don't it's the only thing we want.

It is the same with running. You run because you need to, because you can't imagine living without it, because it brings you joy.

And if you don't miss running the way you miss breathing and drinking, there's no reason you should.

On the Trail with Donald Porter

We might call it *flow* or the *runner's high* or *the joy of running.* Donald Porter calls it *inner running,* that feeling or cluster of feelings that arise with the force

and profundity to make a runner a runner. While each of these terms carries its own flavor, they all privilege therunner's subjective experience above his or her objective achievements. A runner, from this kind of perspective, isn't someone who necessarily runs fast or far but someone who runs because running is a wonderful thing to do.

What distinguishes Porter's inner running is his explicit linking of running and meditation. When approached the right way, "Meditative running can enable you to drop whatever you're clutching for a short time — the beginning of permanent release. It can be a time of day to look at what's happening inside. A time of day to break your normal patterns of obsessive thought. A time to clean your mind, to wash your spirit. Inner running means running for the good feelings associated with it, running for happiness, for joy, for the fun of it."

For many runners this is a common feature of running, but it's one that rarely gets discussed. Luckily for the reader, Porter isn't squeamish around feelings. Running makes him a happier, even a *better*, person; it's no surprise that his enthusiasm for running becomes contagious.

I'd be inclined to call *Inner Running* a forgotten classic, except I can't tell that it was ever known well enough to have been forgotten. None of my runner friends has heard of it, let alone read it. It came into my possession only when my father came across an old mass-market edition in the back of a closet. (My father, not a runner but a student of all things inner, can't recall how he wound up with the book but is certain he never read it — the pristine condition of the spine before I got hold of it attests to this.)

But forgotten or never known, *Inner Running* deserves readers today more than ever. With every $250 Nike shoe guaranteed to make you run faster, with every FitBit or phone app that will quantify and analyze your every bodily movement, with every social media platform asking you to share the details of your run, the pressure for running to be objectified builds and we allow ourselves to be moved further away from the simple fact and joy of being a body in motion.

Trail runners will recognize in themselves a natural affinity for Porter's approach. They are those — *we* are those — who surround ourselves with woods and rivers, with wild animals and cool shade, with desert air and sandy beaches while we play (and for the sake of all things holy, when we're doing it right it is *play*). Where better to appreciate beauty than running alone in nature? Where better to discover a meaningful life with a flourishing person at the center of experience?

And yet isn't trail running becoming more and more about miles and paces and races and elevations and who knows what? Aren't I crossing paths in the woods with more and more runners pushing buttons on gadgets and syncing up devices? More and more runners with phones plugged into their ears. Do they see the bird in the brush? Do they hear the wind through the trees? Do they feel the bliss of existence?

I say *they*, but of course I have myself in mind. It is only because I usually do not see the bird or hear the trees or find existence blissful that it's such a delight when I do. Porter's book is a reminder to these possibilities, a reminder that there are a multitude of ways of relating to our environments and that deliberate attention to one's inner experience while running is one possible way to live a good life.

We runners are lucky for many things. I now count *Inner Running* among these. You'll believe me when I tell you that on this morning's run I ran more slowly than usual, noticed to a new degree the variety of prairie grasses, felt happy and alive and eager for the coming gift of tomorrow's run.

If you are at all inclined toward the mystical, you too will resonate in such moments with Porter, when he writes, "You suddenly experience yourself doing the right thing at the right time for the right reasons; finally you're a round peg in a round hole. The universe is a vast cooperation. Everything's okay the way it is, because it is the way it is."

Runners, go out. And go in.

On My Feet

The blister on my right heel appears only after 10 miles without socks in the red running shoes. But the divot in the callus of my left foot, that seems permanent. While the callus on my left pinky toe grows and recedes as I change from one pair of running shoes to another. My knee pain has vanished as my running shoes have gotten thinner and thinner, although the joints do crackle something structural when I get up in the morning. It's funny the red running shoes are the ones that blister my heel — the flimsy fabric of their heels has itself been ripped apart from use. The white running shoes are too big, and it must be said that wearing them in that marathon was a mistake. The green and yellow running shoes force me to wonder whether I'm quite fast enough to deserve them. Yet they lead me to thoughts of Oregon and Prefontaine, which is maybe why I wear them more than any other pair. The blue running shoes are clunky and I wear them only when my feet are tired and I want to go slow and watch the leaves fall or the ice thaw. When I have the energy, I run barefoot, or close to it, enjoying the feeling of the muscles of my feet flexing in the grass. My latest pair of running shoes had to double as painting shoes and are now caked in globs of white. Maybe they look artsy, hip, like they've been customized by someone with a pop-up boutique. Or maybe I just look like a mess. Probably the latter. But 20 years, how many dozens of shoes, how many thousands of miles, and here I am still putting one foot in front of the other. Still on my feet, whatever's on my feet.

Runner on the Road!

My son learned the word *runner* this month. He's 18 months old. We hike in the mountains every morning. Whenever we cross paths with a runner he takes the opportunity to shout "runner!" with absolute glee. Some runners are out of ear shot before he finds and delivers their label. Others will ignore him. But some will stop and say, "Yes, runner!" or offer a high-five.

When we don't see a runner for a while he will call out from his carrier on my back, "Daddy, run!" This is my cue to take off down the trail. He jostles and bounces and laughs, and when I stop he grants me a short break and then tells me to do it again. The whole month of August is passing us this way. And when I put him down on his own two feet, what do those feet do? Of course, they run. He bounds about and laughs, and if he falls down he gets back up.

It brings such joy to watch a child run, especially one who is just learning. Nietzsche said, "A man's maturity — consists in having found again the seriousness one had as a child, at play."

When I watch my son run, I take pleasure in his delight. I marvel at his discovery and celebration of his body. And I thank him for teaching me again how to run.

Run Away

Barest of bones, what is running? A way of moving from here to there. You've got your legs and your heart and your lungs and not much else to count on. You can cover a lot of ground this way. But there's one thing you can never get away from. No matter how far you run or how fast, you'll find yourself every time already there waiting for you when you stop.

Is this a cruelty or a form of enlightenment? After 20 years of experimentation, I'm inclined to answer this question, "Yes." As long as I keep trying to run away from myself I won't be able to. And as soon as I stop trying I won't need to.

There's no suitable resolution to these paradoxes except to drop them, to walk away, or, better, to run.

———

Scott F. Parker is the author of *A Way Home: Oregon Essays* and *Running After Prefontaine: A Memoir*, among other books. His writing about running has appeared previously in *Sport Literate* as well as online in *Runner's World* and *Running Times* and in the recent book *Hood to Coast Memories*. He teaches writing at Montana State University and runs when he can in the cow pastures outside Bozeman.

Air Ball

—

Jim Daniels

My son got glasses in third grade.
In sixth, he signs up for boys' club hoops.
His wire frames ain't gonna cut it, might
cut *him*. I buy prescription goggles.
Okay so far? No. Despite retrieved images
of Kareem — who *popularized* them, right? —
my son will not wear them. Like Kareem,
he's the tallest. But he cannot shoot a lick,
and maybe if he saw better?

He says he looks goofy, and he does.
Goofy in a serious sports-guy kind of way.
Goofy-scary! *Watch out, sixth graders!*
He wears them once, till one bratty runt
teases him. Remember the great Jabbar —
sky hook, anyone? Just the coach,
and he's the father of the bratty kid.
Expensive. *Prescription*, I repeat.

In the parking lot before the next game,
I hand him the goggles again. He winces.
Da-ad. What's that in his voice?
They got a script for *that*? Voice
changing — it's in the rules. I don
the goggles myself to make a point.
The point is, I see all too clearly.
Hey Kareem — from some old guy
heading into the gym. I mime
a sky hook, an air ball no one sees.

Jim Daniels' recent poetry books include *Rowing Inland* and *Street Calligraphy*, 2017, and *The Middle Ages*, 2018. He is the author of five collections of fiction, four produced screenplays, and has edited five anthologies. Michigan State University Press will publish both his next collection of short fiction, *The Perp Walk*, and his next (coedited) anthology, *R E S P E C T: The Poetry of Detroit Music*, in 2019. He is the Thomas S. Baker University Professor of English at Carnegie Mellon.

L

Charlie, Larry, and Sparrow: A Triptych

—

Barry Peters

bopping	Bird	outside my window
swinging	one-on-one	winging it
groovin high	hands	flitting
fingers flashing	on the ball	bird
on the alto	feints one way	starts
both ways	spins another	stops
far out	feathers	mid-air
improvising	a hook	guile
the wry	look	in his eye
joy	at the brilliance	my eyes rise
skyward	give praise	to the birds

—

Barry Peters, a *Sport Literate* veteran, is a writer and teacher in Durham, North Carolina. His work both appeared in and scheduled for *The American Journal of Poetry, Best New Poets 2018, Miramar, Poetry East, Presence, Rattle, South Florida Poetry Journal*, and *The Southampton Review*.

L

POETRY

At the Health Club

—

David Evans

Over and over day after day, breathing on a treadmill
not far from the basketball court, I'm a witness to
The Golden Rule in Motion, 10 young men taking
their warm-up shots before choosing up sides
for a pick-up game. Friends or strangers —
it doesn't matter — when one of them shoots from
anywhere on the court and makes it, you'd think
the one who got the rebound would be the next
shooter. But instead, the rebounder passes the ball
right back to the shooter: a nice reward for a nice shot.
And it doesn't matter how many shots go in in a row;
whoever gets the rebound automatically feeds the ball
back to the shooter, and the more shots he makes the
more upright he becomes, and the more authentic
the happy-for-you expression on the passer's face,
and the crisper and crisper the passes. But after
a miss, the drama suddenly deflates, and it's anybody's
ball now, with all the freebie shots the shooter must earn
by staying accurate, until he too misses — and takes his
place inside the paint with the other low-key rebounders,
willing not only to receive but also to bestow a kindness.

—

David Evans has had nine poetry collections published. His poems, stories, and essays
have appeared in many magazines and anthologies including *Aethlon: The Journal of Sports
Literature*, *The Norton Book of Sports*, *Splash: Great Writing About Swimming*, and *American
Sports Poems*. He was a Fulbright Scholar twice in China, and a professor and writer-in-
residence at South Dakota State University. He was also poet laureate of South Dakota for
12 years and received the Governor's Award for Creative Achievement in the Arts in 2009.

Battling Battalino

—

Will Stenberg

Featherweight Champion of the World

He boxed for fifteen years, until his hands
were fruit too bruised to sell. Then some tramping
around, a fighter with no fights. He stands
now at the bar, half blind, body cramping.
True, you can always tell an old fighter,
but I know him by more than just his pain.
— After all this, would you do it again?
— A dumb question, you must be a writer.
It's cold and mid-October, and frankly
I have nowhere to go. I fill his cup
and we talk until time itself grows sad.
One more round, then three, and then he thanks me.
Stooped low and low; I bend to sit him up.
— Broken hearts are easy. My hands went bad.

Pete Herman

Will Stenberg

Bantamweight Champion of the World

When Pete Herman turned twelve
his father looked through him
and said — Twelve years lost
so Pete started shining shoes
at a barbershop. Left right left:
another syncopation
in the wild pulse of New Orleans,
the Little-Pete-Herman-Shoeshine Rag.
But there's another use for two hands
that know how to work together.
His boss at the barbershop told him,
— You'll never be a fighter as long as you got
a hole in your ass, but Pete Herman
became the Bantamweight
Champion of the World twice over
fighting Young Zulu,
Little Jack Sharkey,
Kid Williams,
and all it cost him was his left eye,
and his right eye too.

Beau Jack

—

Will Stenberg

Lightweight Champion of the World

Five farm-toughened black children assemble
in a ring: shirtless, eyes shuttered, gloves bulbous
like tubers and ribs that rise. Gathered around
are grown white men, loose ties and untucked shirts.
At the bell, the blindfolded kids begin swinging rough
audacious punches, stumbling, charging, falling.
In the corner is Beau Jack, keeping the ropes to
his back, picking off the other boys as they come
past. The air is hair-grease and cigars. Dimly
through the cloth, like the blind man in the
Gospels who saw men as trees walking, he perceives
strange shapes and cuts them down. Laughter ricochets.
Beau swings, and takes home the money, every night.
From this to a storied career as a champion,
and from that to thirty years as a bootblack
at the Fontaienbleau in Miami Beach, where customers
sometimes call him boy, but the weather is always nice,
and every now and then, from across the lobby
an excited voice says — Hey Champ.

—

Will Stenberg is a writer, musician, and bartender in Portland, Oregon. He records
music under his own name and has also completed a manuscript of boxing poetry,
entitled "No Comebacks," from which these poems are taken. His favorite fighter is
Floyd Patterson.

Catch Up

YOUR LIESURELY
CARRIAGE AWAITS

Sport Literate back issues available online:
www.sportliterate.org

L

ESSAY

A Deep, Sweet Hurt

—

Justina Elias

> Love commingled with hate is more powerful than love. Or hate.
> —Joyce Carol Oates, *On Boxing*

Here's a familiar scene: throngs of people — mostly men — surround a raised platform at the center of an arena. Music thuds, colored lights flare, and one by one, the night's headlining fighters make their entrance. Each is flanked by dozens of wingmen: burly security guys scanning the crowd, cameramen ducking and darting, and a few insiders whose ministrations (mouth guard, water, hug) seem choreographed, swift, and seamless. The "cage," a gleaming black octagon, looms. One fighter drops to her knees and crosses herself before entering; the other, a permanent sneer on her face, just cracks her knuckles mid-stride.

This is where things get less familiar. On tonight's ticket are Joanna Jedrzejczyk and Carla Esparza, strawweights (115 pounds) known, respectively, for striking and grappling prowess. Female MMA fighters have been around since the 19900s, but there's still a thrill in witnessing such unbridled toughness in women. These two are fairly stoic — no strutting or fanged mouth guards à la Amanda "the Lioness" Nunes — but their relative calm only belies a deeper danger. And yet, mouths stuffed with hardware, ribbons in their cornrows, wiry limbs jutting out of board shorts and oversized t-shirts, there is something middle-schoolish about them, a certain uneasy hunger. They eye each other with taut resolve, the world's most devoted bullies.

Round one. The t-shirts have been shed for sports bras but clearly nothing here is meant to titillate; I'm thrown off by the whistles echoing through the crowd. "It's just for the ring girl," my partner assures me, the camera panning to the most familiar scene of all: a bikini model, slim and busty, parading around with a numbered card. "They still have those?" I say ruefully, and we share an uncomfortable laugh. Though the fight itself turns out to be dazzling — a flurry of punches ending in a second-round TKO — it's this moment that will stick with me: the ring girl in her perfect makeup, blowing a kiss to the camera; while behind her Joanna and Carla bump fists, their faces smeared with Vaseline to minimize striking damage.

A few months ago, I was spending a lot of time watching people make cakes. By far the most-lauded feature of the BBC's Great British Bake-Off is its "civility." Contestants compete to become "Britain's best amateur baker," an honor limited to a title and decorative cake plate (no unseemly cash prizes here). Each week's challenges revolve around a theme — "pies," "biscuits," "pastry," etc. — and the bakers tackle them with what seems to be genuine goodwill, often using downtime to help each other roll out dough or assemble gingerbread. The hosts are two chummy female comedians, the judges a hulking celebrity chef and the grandmotherly author of over 70 "cookery books" (her favorite word is "scrummy"), and the whole thing takes place in an airy white tent on the English countryside. Saccharine, yes. But this was November 2016: we were all hungry for civility.

So how did I get here, tearing through the archives of UFC's Fight Pass?

Like Bake-Off, part of MMA's appeal is its simplicity. Not in execution — landing the perfect hook is every bit as complicated as mixing a perfect meringue — but purpose: take your opponent down using whatever means you can. Almost. Initially the sport allowed for eye gouging and crotch shots, but like boxed mixes in Bake-Off, cheap shortcuts of this ilk were soon nixed for PR reasons. Still, the rules are shockingly sparse compared to other combat sports. Competitors can punch, kick, knee, elbow, tackle, and choke; most notoriously, hitting a grounded opponent isn't off-limits. It sounds cruel until you actually watch someone maneuver out of a so-called "ground-and-pound" attack; if fighters train for it, the argument goes, why not let them test their skills?

For mindless violence this is not. The (aptly-named) *Guardian* may condemn "the calculated brutality of this so-called 'sport,'" but it's those very calculations that make it sport: as blood pours from the slashed scalp of bantamweight Joe Soto, commentators gravely note that the decreased friction will hinder his opponent's submission attempts. Heartless, maybe, but when medics rush in at the end of the fight, Soto's too busy running victory laps to let them bandage the wound. "He knew what he was getting into," my partner shrugs.

It's true: fighters choose to endanger themselves, a choice so beyond comprehension to many that it tends to get overlooked. And it's on this point that I find myself in strangely familiar territory. Traditional critiques of blood sport decry what Joyce Carol Oates describes as its "'vicious exploitation of maleness' as prostitution and pornography may be said to be a vicious exploitation of femaleness" — and just as such blanket dismissal downplays sex workers' agency, it reduces skilled fighters to helpless pawns, duped and victimized. "If this had occurred in the street," the aforementioned *Guardian* article continues, "the public's reaction would be one of horror and revulsion." "Yeah," a commenter swiftly retorts, "it's almost like things like context and mutual consent make a difference!"

Of course, in MMA as in sex work, neither context nor consent is simple (though UFC fighters skew whiter and are generally more privileged than, say, boxers). Still, even a nod to the concepts is conspicuously absent from the moralizing op-eds I find everywhere from *Salon* to *The New York Times*. As I scroll through articles condemning the sport's brutality, its baseness, its incongruity with civilized society, I can't help but wonder how these same largely liberal publications would approach BDSM or other marginalized sexual practices. For like pearl-clutching homophobes, naysayers seem more interested in unpleasant bodily details than they are in the nuances of their subjects' lived reality.

And there *are* nuances. Beyond logistics, beyond risk. For example: if MMA is, at its core, a cult of brutish masculinity, what does it mean when women enter that hallowed realm?

I was wrong about Joanna's stoicism. Turns out she's famous for trash talking, for ducking to force her opponent's lowered eyes into a staredown, for draping her blood-spattered body in the Polish flag like a warlord. My favorite quirk is the way she raises her index finger for "number one," an image that can't help but evoke Catholic iconography; with her sunken eyes and bony body (the weight cuts are famously grueling for her) she could be a medieval saint, hand raised in benediction.

Self-mortification, of course, is the name of the game in combat sport. Beyond the toils of fighting itself are those of training, shaping oneself toward a painfully precise target. Yet this degree of self-scrutiny doesn't seem so alien to me; swap out the male boxer with any woman, fighter or no, and the following passage from Oates' *On Boxing* could read as feminist commentary:

Like a dancer, a boxer 'is' his body, and is totally identified with it.
And the body is identified with a certain weight.

The crucial difference is that weight in this context isn't some nebulous marker of virtue but a concrete step toward victory; losing it is "part of the job," transparently deliberate. Gone is the goal of making one's physique look effortless — the rigors of exercise and the agonies of dieting are all part of the fighter's mythology. Joanna leaves the gym in tears of exhaustion every day; Ronda Rousey sits in a sauna for five hours to shed water; Cristiane "Cyborg" Justino lies on the floor weeping after a hard indoor run in winter layers. Outside the structure of sport these actions sound pitiable, grounds for intervention. Here, like the anorexia of centuries past, they're sacrifice made spectacle, all in service of a greater glory.[1]

And it's this — the glory of it all — that seems to me the crucial distinction between fighting and sex work: that most feminized, least glorified form of bodily currency. Fighters risk life and limb for money, yes, but the naked joy on Joanna's face the moment she wins the championship is one of self-possession. Yet watching her straddle the edge of the cage, her ropey arms flexed in victory, I'm equal parts gleeful and wary, already steeling myself for the usual media takedown. I've witnessed the body-shaming thrown at Rousey, seen the way the UFC has marketed female fighters in heels and miniskirts, cringed at nicknames like the "Karate Hottie" given to fellow strawweight Michelle Waterson. The ways in which female athletes are expected to compensate for their power (makeup, sexy photo shoots, frequent references to male partners) are well-documented, and it seems impossible that Joanna's body will remain subject rather than object in the public eye. When I google *Joanna Jedrzejczyk sexist*, half the results are for "sexiest."

And yet, though only seven years have passed since UFC president Dana White claimed women would never fight under his organization's banner, public discussion around female fighters isn't all so retrograde. Rousey remains one of the only MMA fighters in the world to have gained "household name" status (through the UFC, at that), and I'm bolstered to find a study on Polish coverage of Joanna in *The Journal of Sport and Social Issues* that reveals:

a general tendency to describe her — and her fights — in ways which depart from the traditional discursive feminization of female athletes;

to praise her physical and mental qualities as a champion fighter; and

to hold Jedrzejczyk up as a symbol of national pride.

The same paper notes a surprising receptiveness to "Joanna Champion's" self-confidence. "I have told you that I will win and I have just done it," she pants, beaming, in a typical post-fight interview. The accent helps (at least to Western ears), as does her size. For she is, however powerful, *small*, and there's a familiar sweetness to that incongruity: everyone loves a tomboy. To watch a scowling Ronda Rousey, 20 pounds heavier and correspondingly busty, tug at her spaghetti straps before a fight is to witness a more disheartening struggle:

---

1 I would be remiss in failing to mention Rousey's now well-known history of bulimia — certainly not one of the strategies highlighted in promo material. Still, the process doesn't seem much more gruesome than some of the others mentioned here. How might we respond, a part of me wonders, to sticking a finger down one's throat if public consciousness of the practice had begun with male boxers and not female pop stars?

that of a woman who'll never be described as "girlish" or "scrappy," a woman whose power and sexuality are equally visible and, to many, intrinsically opposed. I click on another Joanna fight, eager to shake off these doubts. It's the closest match I've seen yet — no thrilling KOs, just relentless knees and elbows to the legs, belly, face — but by the end, like Carla Esparza and Jessica Penne before her, challenger Valerie Letourneau is clearly the worse for wear. Despite it going to decision, the action has been riveting, but as with the Esparza fight it's a peripheral moment that haunts me. The fight is over; teams swarm the cage; Joanna is coolly victorious, a tiny cut on her forehead the only hint of a struggle. Meanwhile, a battered Valerie turns away from her posse, bracing herself against the cage. She's taken 258 strikes (she landed less than half that) but her body tells a clearer story than any scorecard — her legs are bruised, her chest gleams with blood, and a darkening goose egg above her right cheekbone is already so puffy it could be an eyepatch. Stubbornly she holds her arms up, fending off her well-meaning teammates, but as the camera pans right it's impossible not to notice the horde of photographers just opposite the cage. There's an old axiom about fighting: you can't run and you can't hide.

What do we talk about when we talk about women's anger?

We know our place. We're the gossipers, the eye rollers, the silent sufferers; we take classes for self-defense, then smile to keep from having to use them. Boys are the ones whose wounds run skin deep, who clap each other on the back after schoolyard brawls. We swallow our grievances, keep on smiling, rot from the inside out.

So yes, it's cathartic watching two women beat the shit out of each other.

But it isn't just that. Professional fighting is, as Oates puts it, "primarily about being, and not giving, hurt" — the former being a (typically lengthy) prerequisite to the latter. And that seems right to me. Famous as male stoicism may be, women are the ones — not to get too essentialist about it — who move through life under the specter of childbirth, that ultimate arc of fear, pain, and triumph. And a lifetime of self-policing seems to me an appropriate background for a sport based largely on mental mastery. Be aware of your surroundings, pay attention to body language, watch yourself, watch yourself — we're all a mouth-guard away, it seems, from the mantras of the training gym.

Still, though we're perfectly comfortable letting women suffer in private, the spectacle MMA makes of pain is too much for many to take. It's not just the risk but the frankness with which the sport approaches injury that makes it so unpalatable — otherwise we'd ban cheerleading and skiing with the same verve. To enter the cage is to enter kink territory, a sanctified space in which people choose to hurt under their own terms. And like responsible dominatri-ces, those inflicting pain in a professional fight are only mimicking heedlessness: high-caliber fighting, with its infinite calculations, transcends anything so blinding as rage.

It's not a perfect parallel. While both doms and fighters monitor their partners closely, the former are responsible for ending things when the pain is too much. Fighters have the luxury of outsourcing this task to the ref. For women, it's a role reversal that feels both novel and ancient: gone is the Victorian "angel in the house," that civilizing presence who transcends the pulls of the flesh; in her place is a medieval conception of the female, a beastly figure whose urges must be tempered by more disciplined men. But these are animal instincts honed by years of conscious training: all that time spent for a taste of timelessness, the freedom of a cage. In so many ways it's a Gothic sport, for all its apparent directness. Contradictions haunt every fight, shadows in deadlock. No ref or timer to force them apart, pretend there's such thing as an answer.

I've been reading a lot about doublethink this year. And haunting. If it's a strange time to be an American it may be stranger still to feel yourself so dismayed by the politics of a country that isn't, technically, your own. You'd think we'd be used to it by now. But I'm not sure Canadians ever get used to standing in this shadow: enjoying its coolness, denying its darkness.

In the time since I started writing this, former MMA star War Machine (his legal name as of 2008) has been found guilty on 29 of 34 charges of assault, kidnapping, and myriad other offences against his ex-girlfriend, porn star Christy Mack. It's disturbing to see the power gap between sex workers and fighters so cartoonishly illustrated, more disturbing yet to learn that, according to a 2014 report by HBO, domestic violence rates among MMA fighters are as much as double that of the general population. Like rape apologists the world over, Dana White has claimed that fighters "don't bounce back" from such accusations while blatantly disproving that stance: from Todd Stoute to Kyacey Uscola to Cody East (to name just a few), convicted abusers and rapists continue to be embraced by the UFC. It's naïve of me, maybe, to find any of this surprising, but weeks focusing on women's fighting, on artful commentary more concerned with the sublime transmutations of the cage than the disinhibiting effects of routine head trauma (not to mention steroid abuse, homophobia, etc…) have left me with a rosier view of the sport than it may deserve. Looking around at the largely white, largely male audience in our local sports bar — bellowing at our harried-looking waitress for more tequila — I can't help but wonder how they vote.

And so I find myself, again, in familiar territory. It's the same path I took with "sex positivity," that stubbornly sunny stance so often at odds with real-world inequalities. As with sex work, my problem with MMA is not one of ideology but culture: the intricacies of a fight itself may preclude unconsidered rage, but Christy Mack's wounded body proves that that rage isn't without other channels. And like johns for whom consent is irrelevant, a public willing to shrug off such abuse for a few hours' entertainment makes it hard to maintain that the latter has nothing to do with the former.

Or maybe the very brazenness of that disregard is part of MMA's draw. No breezy white tents or feel-good formulas here to mask the persistent reek of toxic masculinity. If Bake-Off's treacly politeness seems at odds with a post-Brexit Britain, at least the UFC is right on track with recent American history: a man's world in which women's wellbeing takes a backseat to showmanship; a world in thrall to ritual, to "beasts," "predators," "monsters." Some of whom — bafflingly, thrillingly — are women themselves.

Is this the real joy of it: watching women fight their way through the ranks of such a bluntly male universe? More than one commentator has called Joanna "the best striker in the game" — no gendered qualifier. Maybe I should know better, in 2018, than to put my faith in that excellence, to assume that if only they're tough enough, strong enough, women can chip away at even the deepest-set misogyny. Still, I can't help but hope. It's sickening, it's thrilling, it's suicide, it's rebirth: it's the drive to lock yourself in a cage knowing you'll get punched in the face — and the drive to keep on punching back, even as you fall.

This essay first appeared in *Under the Gum Tree*.

———

Justina Elias holds an MFA in Creative Writing from the University of Guelph. Her work has appeared in *Room Magazine, The Puritan*, and *Under the Gum Tree*. She has been a finalist in contests with *Narrative, Glimmer Train, the CBC*, and *Room*. She works as a bookseller on Canada's west coast.

A Fight Club You'll Want to Talk About

"Let's get ready to **DISCUSS TOXIC MASCULINITY!**"
Renew your subscription, subscribe anew, or pick up a
copy of our Fall 2019 "Fight Club" issue online.

Featuring roundhouse essays from Justina Elias, Mark Anthony
Jarman, Lois Melina, Dave Murphy, and John Julius Reel (to name
a fearsome five) and impactful poetry from John Belk, Dorothy
Dickinson, Ken Ferrell, Adam Hughes, Matthew Johnson, Eddie
Krzemski, and Will Stenberg (to name seven sluggers). Plus our
"Fight Contest" poetry and essay winners.

Boxing

M.G. Stephens

1.

Mike you dirty Irish bastard
He would say when he called me
On the telephone
To see when we could hang out

And he would come to my flat
On 110th Street in Morningside Heights
Where I made him a tuna fish
Sandwich and we watched old fights

He was Billy Graham
Irish Billy Graham a welterweight
They called him to distinguish
Him from the evangelist

And Billy once told me a story
About a fight he had in the
Coney Island Velodrome
Losing every round

Because he wouldn't listen
To his cornerman and trainer
Whitey Bimstein who told him
To move to the right or left

In order to stop being hit
By his opponent but Billy
Balked and didn't listen
And stood there slugging it out

2.

Whitey Bimstein his manager
Pleaded with his fighter Billy Graham
Round after round
Please Billy please he said

Just move to the right
Move a fuckin' inch to the right
So that this bastard will stop
Punching the shit out of you

But Billy being a stubborn Irishman
(his father Pop Graham was Scottish
And his mother came from Limerick)
Refused to budge for his opponent

And yet Billy went out there in the
Seventh round moved an inch to the right
Threw a left hook and knocked
Out this opponent

And in his corner Whitey Bimstein
Danced a jig that his fighter
Finally listened to his advice
And knocked out the bum

The moral of the story Billy asked me
The moral of the story
Then he laughed and said
How the fuck should I know

M.G. Stephens is author of 22 books, including the critically acclaimed novel *The Brooklyn Book of the Dead*; the travel memoir *Lost in Seoul* (Random House, 1990); and the award-winning essay collection *Green Dreams*. His boxing novel *Kid Coole* is looking for a home, and big parts of it were serialized in the *Brooklyn Rail* magazine a few years ago. After living in London for many years, he currently resides north of Chicago.

L

POETRY

Our Hall of Fame

———

Eric Chiles

The letter didn't come from Canton
or Cooperstown but the principal
of our high school. I had ignored
an earlier email as a gimmick
to open my checkbook, but this
was personally signed, inviting
me and the other members
of our wrestling team, which won
three consecutive state titles,
to a reception and induction
before a basketball game.

Someone had found our trophies
and banners in a closet under
fifty years of debris. A custodian
almost threw them in a dumpster,
but the current coach recognized
a motivational opportunity.

Halls of Fame are serious honors.
They make you remember what
you once had, and their mention
makes obituaries more interesting.

Two thirds of our team showed up,
although, sadly a few had lost life's
last bout. Jude died years ago
from brain cancer. Louie, one of our
lightweights, struggled with sobriety
and succumbed to booze. Mike,

my practice partner, and a college
champ, a children's home director
who consoled my wife and I
during the trials of adolescence
and liked his bourbon on the rocks
despite kidney disease, dropped dead
on the retirement community golf course
while playing a round with his wife.

Bobby, who had defeated an opponent
who later put Slippery Rock on the map
and medaled at the Olympics
became a high-wire ironworker in California,
and our heavyweight, John, who last
I heard was a lobsterman in Maine,
didn't make the trip.

None of us who did come could
make weight today, although, Tim
was closest. He wore the blazer
the school bought us after we won
the second championship in 1966.
I'm sizes past fitting in mine.
He also had a scrapbook tracing
all our exploits from CYO through
that last tournament in Lancaster.
What a collection of yellowed memories.

He and Gene talked about operating
cranes at the long-shuttered steel mill.
Jim talked about not being able
to get to the NCAA tournaments
anymore because they're held
on the weekend he opens his
Italian ice stand for the season.
Bruce, who wrestled 106 pounds,
is now as tall as me, the 154 pounder.
Greg who wrestled the weight below
me, and got better every year, drove
up from Virginia where he still
practices law. I hadn't seen him

since graduation, and while we
were competitors then, there
was the sense that night we could
have become better friends.

None of us will ever step on the mat
again and probably won't see each
other before the final fall.

———

Eric Chiles, a former career journalist, is an adjunct professor of journalism and English at a number of colleges and universities in eastern Pennsylvania. His poetry appears in *Allegro, American Journal of Poetry, Chiron Review, Gravel, Plainsongs, Rattle, San Pedro River Review, Tar River Poetry, Third Wednesday,* and other journals. His chapbook *Caught in between* is forthcoming from Desert Willow Press.

POETRY

Fairbanks 1980

———

Rob Greene

When I was six Larry Holmes was my favorite
before he took an aging Ali down,
punching Ali and punching Ali
while telling the ref to stop the fight
similar to the time my overworked airman father
punched me in the face
when I went over to hug him goodnight
while he was busying himself in between
swing shifts by taping his vinyl records
until one skipped a beat
when I opened the stereo cabinet glass.

Those were the good days, the days
when I took his best punch and got up without crying
just like Ali took Holmes's best.
That summer I made a kite during a short stint
in the Webelos, a paper kite with my drawing
of Larry Holmes and my dad on the back facing skyward
in repentance to the Alaskan sun.

———

Rob Greene is the editor of *Raleigh Review* and he is a doctoral candidate and post-graduate researcher with University of Birmingham [United Kingdom] as well as an assistant professor at Saint Augustine's University in Raleigh, North Carolina. He has a recent poem in the Berlin based annual *Herzattacke*, and others in *Poem of the Week, Open Minds Quarterly, Great River Review,* and *WLA: War, Literature & the Arts*. Greene relocated 46 times prior to moving to Raleigh close to two decades ago.

L

POETRY

Tennis Whites at Booker T. Washington

—

Markham Johnson

Royce hates tennis, but loves to smack
crisp suburban boys with fuzzy yellow

balls. *Stay the fuck away from my net.* He mouths
these words as our opponents rub

red welts. He doesn't look back when I laugh,
but it's 1972, and I'm the one white kid

playing tennis for Booker T. Washington. *Serve,
Johnson,* he nods, linebacker hands squeezing

steel racket. At singles, we fail: ground
strokes, like purple martins chase

mayflies, passing shots clang off posts
one court over. Even in doubles,

Royce and I must win points early, losing
long rallies to teams dressed in IZOD.

My serve is flat and hard, peeling
paint from worn cement, so the return wobbles

across the net to Royce. *Yes,* he grins, while skinny
boys on the other side, swear fidelity

to the goddess of segregated schools, unsure
which body part to protect.

They would flee, but fathers in bleachers
are leaning in as my partner raises his Wilson T2000

to invoke 300 years of revenge. Royce,
I still recall the joy of playing on your side.

Markham Johnson's poems have appeared in many literary magazines, and his first book, *Collecting the Light*, was published by the *University Press of Florida*. In 2016, he won the Pablo Neruda Prize from *Nimrod*, and he holds an MFA from Vermont College. For the past 20 years, he has been a teacher at Holland Hall in Tulsa, Oklahoma, where he has also coached baseball, basketball, and tennis.

L

POETRY

Moses and Zipporah Attend
a Roller Derby Game

——

Crystal Stone

He and Zipporah drank brandy hot chocolates
and ate blueberries on the floor by the space heater.
It was winter. Zipporah was bored so she melted
pencils in the tea candle lights they had in the window
until Moses hid them from her. "Please," she asked.
"Can we go to the roller derby this time?"
He was always busy: extinguishing burning bushes,
delivering commandments to local courthouses, parting
the red sea, but when their own oven caught
flames, she had to take care of it herself — the wall
still scarred black from smoke. Moses didn't mind;
in his 96th year, appearances meant little to him.
His wife's love meant much more. "I will
give it a try tonight." He preferred the quiet
nights at home holding hands, but he saw the way
she rushed to change into something more festive
and knew it was the right time to buy tickets.
The sight was jarring: he had never known women
to be so violent — not even his wife who cheered
shamelessly as the visiting team's jammer took
a knee, struggling to get up after a large blow.
She daydreamed about wearing the star herself,
but she never had the courage to try. How
would it reflect on her husband if she took pleasure
taking and giving hits? Wearing fishnets in public?
The patterns on their tights resembled the sand
at the bottom of the red sea. If only she could part
with comfort, divinity, purpose and for a few hours
let the wheels roll her somewhere else, in circles,

where she wouldn't be a wife or a mother
where god wouldn't be the announcer calling her
moves. She could pretend, for a minute, god wouldn't
know her every thought or desire, the knowledge
he possessed without her verbal consent. "If I were
a derby girl, my name would be zip-through-her."
She smiled, threw back her $1 beer. *How strange*
Moses thought. *To love someone and never*
know how much they might want something else.

Crystal Stone's poetry has previously appeared or is forthcoming in *Collective Unrest, Driftwood Press, Anomaly, New Verse News, Occulum, BONED, Eunoia Review, isacoustics, Tuck Magazine, Writers Resist, Drunk Monkeys, Coldnoon, Poets Reading the News, Jet Fuel Review, Sigma Tau Delta Rectangle, North Central Review, Badlands Review, Green Blotter, Southword Journal Online* and *Dylan Days*. She is currently pursuing her MFA at Iowa State University, gave a TEDx talk on poetry, and her first collection of poetry, *Knock-Off Monarch*, was recently released from Dawn Valley Press.

L

POETRY

Beer League

——

Matt Robinson

Rudy's always ready near two hours early — smooth-sweatered,
laced, & taped all wrist-rigid —way, way goddamned prior
to his scheduled ice; the sweaty-canned ire of others
whose rooms he's quick-claimed & bench-annexed as much
of a sweat-starting balm as any Lifebrand, tube-smeared,
old-man-with-the-knee-smelling crap he's slathered on
rink-bound from nearby Giant Tiger, or Shopper's, or his wife's
bathroom sink's drawer.   But despite what you'd think
after dour CBC specials or those ad-ridden clickbaits
linked on the Facebook by your uncle or aunt or
that guy-from-your-high-school whose girl winked your way
knowingly at that decades-past prom, this whole stinking
ritual has next to nothing — *no, nothing* — to do
with the cancer, with how his body's gone wrong. The man's
simply earnest, eager, full of a vinegared piss. He's not
pseudo-religiously locker-shotgunning these Friday nights' rooms;
there's no penance in this watching a ponderous Zamboni
driver's near-inert thrumming, still short a lazy, penultimate circuit
or two. The guy simply eschews most players' preferred,
pre-game approach, wherein one's tardily coaxing the dull ache
of a newly-tweaked hammy or easing their Bud-bloated ab
through the mouldering wait of moist pants like the sloughed-off dun
slush numbly gate-shoveled across a post-boards abyss
as the buzzer alarums the 3-minute warning & the stripes
strategize their next on-ice blitzed fuckery. Rudy's good
in the room: luckily fine with shortish shifts here & there;
the odd second assist or beery catheter crack, some off-colour bluster
around ill-fitting diapers or a swollen ballsack that'll barely fit
the new cup he just grabbed off of Bubba at SportChek
for a fraction of what it *really should've cost him*. At one point

we'd lost him — we'd thought — to oncologist's blades, but
then he was back, early & eager. Again bent & beleaguered,
wrought forearms all tense with looming skate laces, the room's dank safety net.
That interwoven, unspoken collection of faces.

———

Matt Robinson's *no cage contains a stare that well* (ECW, 2005) is a full-length
collection of poems exploring the game of hockey. His most recent publications are
the chapbooks *Against* (Gaspereau, 2018) and *The Telephone Game* (Baseline, 2017),
as well as the trade collection *Some Nights It's Entertainment; Some Other Nights
Just Work* (Gaspereau, 2016). Previous collections include *a fist made and then un-
made* (Gaspereau, 2013), which was short-listed for the bpNichol Award, as well
as *Against the Hard Angle* (ECW, 2010) and *A Ruckus of Awkward Stacking* (Insomniac,
2000). He lives in Halifax, Nova Scotia, with his family, and plays goal in the HRHL,
one of Halifax's best beer leagues, where he occasionally stops a few pucks and regularly
drinks a few beers.

A Mother's Ode to the Zamboni

—

Sarah Key

Between periods a mother re-surfaces,
takes a breath while you chug over blood,

broken sticks, lost mouth guards, sweeping it all
your shavers sashay your name sweet as
Tyrolean pastry, Zamboni, Zamboni,

make your getaway clean, leave us a sheet
not to settle old scores, but to smooth a new course

while you spray   a break
in the glide   no bodies collide

you flush and you shush the ice for its
surfers. Between what periods does a mother

get away clean? Her sheets
soak it all up as you hum she laces
her thoughts around once-tiny feet

inhales your fumes catching her breath
her breath ever catching.

—

Sarah Key, since retiring as a hockey mom, has had a few dozen poems published in print and online, the latest being her muscle-car poem in *CALYX* and a villanelle in the Spring 2018 issue of *The Georgia Review*. She is in four anthologies, including *Nasty Women Poets*. Her creative writing life began in entertainment public relations where she learned to write pure fiction. She has written eight cookbooks and essays for the *Huffington Post*. Her students at a community college in the South Bronx are her favorite teachers.

EVERYONE A SWIMMER

A short film by Steve Mend, written by William Meiners

Adolph Kiefer, perhaps the greatest American swimmer you've never heard of, won gold in the 1936 Olympics. In one of his last interviews, the near centenarian shared his remarkable life story with us.

 Literate

Go online to sportliterate.org and "K" for "Kiefer" in the "A to Z" links.

L

ESSAY

Shooting a Deer

—

Amy Jenkins

He's not really my uncle, but I call him Uncle Bill. He's been my Aunt Lil's boyfriend for a dozen years. Bill is a carpenter, mason, electrician, and hunter. Hard of hearing, he just starts up a-talkin' about what's on his mind rather than responding to a conversation. "She come up from the swamp and raised her nose in the air. Bow pierced her heart; she went down quick."

He chewed swamp-doe venison sausage while he talked. My up-north Wisconsin relatives spend their November vacations and weekends in the swamps and fields of northeastern Wisconsin. The meat is important to their winter diet, so all are thankful that the chronic wasting disease that has infected other parts of the state's deer population, has not been found in Marinette County. My relatives wouldn't starve without the venison, but the hunt, the freezers and mason jars of venison steaks and roasts, and the recipes for cooking the lean protein are essential to the up-north culture. Our German and English ancestors came to this land based on the promise of land, game, and a kind of freedom that feels related to what goes on between humanity and the forest.

When I was a young girl, my parents made perennial November drives from Milwaukee to the land where my mother had hunted and dogged every autumn in her memory. When I was about nine, they taught me to dog; I never carried a gun but helped the hunters with my little-girl squeal. Relatives who knew the terrain chose a square of land. Eight to 10 of us, dogs and hunters alike got in line, yelping and stomping to flush out deer, while other hunters stood in watchful wait.

The woods were cold, but my belly was warm with eggs, hash browns, and fried ham and bacon. We even ate apple pie. Since it was Grandpa's breakfast favorite and apples were easy to find on abandoned land that had once been farmed by families, everyone got a pass to eat pie with eggs. Along with parents and grandparents, aunts, uncles, cousins, and hunting pals, we all gorged on a big old farm breakfast. These folks were bonded by their familiarity with 4 a.m. farm mornings, and hunting further bonded the group as providers of meat for the family. In our family, the men and women hunted, and that was also a source of pride for me. That kitchen was wood-stove warm, smelled of coffee and fried bacon, and rattled with the chatter of hunting plans. They used specialized words I didn't understand.

"If we drive the Spikehorn, Evie can use her old stand — where she shot the eight-point year before last."

"The road off the Long Slide's been showing activity."

"You using the 30 ought 6, or going back to the McMillan?"

They sounded competent and excited, chewin' and fast talkin' at the yellow aluminum-edged table.

Before daybreak, we were in the swamp. Walking through plots of November swampland was toe-numbing cold. Sometimes the swamp water crusted with a skin of ice that broke when I stepped on it. Each step brought a moment of security, then a two-inch, or six-inch, or even eight-inch plunge into chilly swamp water. I always worried my foot would go 10-feet deep, and I'd be screaming and going under like a quicksand victim, and they'd all think 'What a good dog she is; wow what a screamer.'

Those hunters weren't worried. Even though I usually couldn't see them, an adult on each side of me tracked my pace on the line. They wouldn't let me get a step ahead. They knew the land, woods, and names of the trees, birds, rocks, moss, and animal tracks. I loved being in the woods, the realm of my relatives. I loved the stories at the end of the drive about who had seen what, the foxes, hares, pileateds and other exotics that had escaped my gaze. Often, they'd ask if I'd seen the young doe, old buck, or fox that passed in front of me. No, I generally only noticed my feet as I struggled through the rough terrain.

On a later drive, after it began to snow, watching my feet evolved into watching for animal tracks. I recognized rabbit tracks, followed by what Grandpa later confirmed were bobcat tracks. Both sets of tracks grew farther apart, and I understood I was following the chase, and I was a part of the chase. The bobcat tracks disappeared many feet before the creek, echoing a deathblow pounce. In the middle of a small stream, a snow-covered boulder held a pool of fresh, bright blood, and one set of tracks leading away. My nine-year-old self-imagined a dead bunny, but I couldn't deny the excitement of being so close to the pursuit. I imagined that bobcat, the soft white-spotted fur, the three soft pads of the paws moving silently through the swamp and woodland. I was working to make peace with the small scene before me. I began to appreciate the beauty in the blood on the snow when I noticed our entire dog line had halted. Mom, 20 yards to my left, made crossing-guard arms to me; the message — stand still.

I saw him, his shiny brown eyes, his moist nose that rose up from the ground and twitched before he turned his 10-point rack away from me and darted. The shot detonated my stillness. Everyone started moving, and I got the arm wave to pick up my pace.

I thought they missed him because he ran and leapt into my view three more times before he dropped. We followed the blood trail. The shooter yelled from up ahead. "He's a beauty!" I caught up to the hustle and stories of the kill. They posed with him, took pictures, and pulled up his head by the rack, so I could see how he'd have looked lying on the forest floor listening for danger.

He was beautiful.

He was dead.

I stood in the background of the scene and watched them cut into his belly, release the steaming warmth that had been life, and pull the slippery red and blue entrails out onto the frozen woodland. Snot and tears froze to my face. I have always remembered that scene, and how confusing and sad it was to see those details of life and death.

I never dogged with the hunters again, always found excuses, spent my Novembers in the city, never graduated from dog to hunter. I just couldn't watch, couldn't yell, and couldn't shoot.

With his mouth full of swamp doe, Uncle Bill had evoked images of that hunting kill, and I refused a slice of venison sausage, perched on a Ritz, for emotional rather than logical reasons. Uncle Bill chomped as he left the kitchen to bring in more firewood.

Uncle Bill had bought 40 acres of land with money he earned from decades of skilled manual labor. He cleared a section of forest to build a cabin from the very trees he'd cut. At over 75 years old, he did it all himself. He felled each tree and hauled the logs to the sawmill and back. He nailed each nail, ran the electricity, and laid the stone fireplace. Although he had Aunt Lil select the arrangement of the green, beige, blue and grey stones, citing "What the hell do I know about color coordination?"

Uncle Bill took us all out to the almost finished cabin on our most recent up-north trip. About 25 relatives were there; all the local families were hunters. All were February festive without a holiday to celebrate: cooking, playing games, sledding, taking the kids on snowmobile rides, making a racket of jokes, laughing at the baby giggle, and teasing each other. Aunt Lil told about the unfinished ceiling. "Bill laid pine boards on the floors and walls. He was going to lay them on the ceiling, but I told him he might have too much to drink, and not know where to walk.

We were a noisy bunch, except at one window that faced a field. "Look." Five-year-old Abbey's finger pointed out the window, and her small voice and stillness hushed us. Five deer moved slowly toward tan piles in the snow. A quiet voice behind me explained. "Bill feeds them hay and corn." By this late in winter, food's scarce. Lots of deer don't make it through the long winters. He's got names for the regulars. He even picked up a glass storm door from the dump and put it on the outhouse, so he can watch them from where he sits after morning coffee.

The day and evening stayed fun and noisy, but everyone took at least one turn at the quiet window. These deer and venison lovers have an honest relationship with their prey. I glimpsed it before we ate our potluck dinner.

Asking God to "bless our food" changed meaning for me. I always thought it was about me, like "Thanks for feeding me" or "Don't let this food give me gastritis," or even "Let it nourish me, so I might serve you." I never understood the direct meaning of "bless our food," like my up-north relatives do. They understand the sacrifice of the deer.

———

Amy Lou Jenkins is a writer, speaker and educator. She is the recipient of a Mesa Refuge Writing Fellowship. Her book, *Every Natural Fact Five Seasons of Open-Air Parenting* won the Ellis /Henderson Award for Outdoor Writing and Living Now US Book Award. She holds an MFA from Bennington and teaches writing at universities, conferences, and workshops. Her work has appeared in *The Florida Review*, *Earth Island Journal*, *Rosebud*, *Wisconsin Trails*, *Wisconsin People and Ideas*, *Big Apple Parent*, *Women on Writing*, *Wild with Child*, *The Maternal is Political*, and more. She served as editor and contributor for *Corners: Voices on Change*. More at www.AmyLouJenkins.com.

L

POETRY

Inheritance

———

Caroline Collins

In their time, my mother's people
were famous for their fishing
in the Mississippi river bottoms,
their names now put down in books.
My mother sat us on the bank one day
with nightcrawlers and canepoles,
showed us how it worked. With her help,
I managed a tiny bluegill,
which my great-grandfather praised.

But I never quite got the hang of it,
despite all those hours of waiting
for the cork to wobble and go under,
never developed the agile wrist
for bringing the pole up and in
or the patience to keep trying.
I let the dark water lull me to sleep.

At home on the porch, my mother
lifted each fish from the stringer,
wielded the board, the flashing knife
and the nail, scraped the guts into a bucket
and tossed the bladders at us
("floaters" she'd played with as a girl),
laughing when we dodged and yelped.

Now they have entered the boat
together and untied it,
my mother and her weathered grandfather,
dropping nets and scattering chum,

fishing in heaven and laughing
while I go on here, putting out lines
and waiting, trying hard
to snag something worthwhile,
always fishing for words.

———

Caroline Collins holds an MFA in creative writing and a doctoral degree in 19th Century American Literature from the University of Arkansas. Her poems have appeared in a number of literary journals, including *Calyx*, *Mochila Review*, *Shenandoah*, and *Southern Poetry Review*. Her collection of poetry, *Presences*, was published by Parallel Press, an imprint of the University of Wisconsin Press, in 2014. Other poems have appeared recently in *The Lindenwood Review*. She currently teaches first-year writing, American literature, and creative writing at Gordon State College in Barnesville, Georgia.

Everyone's Portrait as Aaron Rodgers

—

Kate Wright

Sagittarius, hot headed
fire signs with an ego problem,
we're crazy — you can see it
in our eyes. We yell at the receivers
when they drop a pass, we don't talk
to our brother, and we dog-shame
our dog on Facebook when it has an accident
on the rug. We trust our friends even if they're bad people —
will bet millions of dollars on their "cleanness"
even when we know we probably shouldn't.
We get mad at the team when they release our best friend.
They release our best friend because we demand
a bigger paycheck. We meditate, do yoga,
meet the Dali Lama and give him a Packers hat.
We smile for the press. Miss America wants us
to call her. We don't. We tell the fans to "relax",
but we don't get to. We eat salad. We break up
with our girlfriend. We cut out cheese
and drinking and the rest of our family. We take care
of our self and our multi-million-dollar arm.
We're tired. The receivers don't invite us to play
Settlers of Catan. 82,000 eyes watch us take the field.
We're surrounded by people but we're all alone.

Gymnasts' Salute

After "Dolor" by Theodore Roethke

Kate Wright

I have known the secret sadness of leotards,
tight on the bodies of girls who no longer wish to wear them,
the frustration of falling, arched backs, bent arms, and flexed feet,
all the anguish of blood staining the chalky hand red,
exasperation of joints and muscles seizing
with lactic acid, the need to keep going,
the humiliation of supports, sports tape, and braces,
shame in sitting to the side, head in hands.
And I have seen the endless parade of children's faces
twist and contort to a false maturity,
forced smiles turn to wide-eyed
fear, to teeth-gritted grief, confess
to the coach, tongue heavy with the doctor's orders,
walk, limp, crutch through the gym door.

Kate Wright received her BA and MA in English from Penn State University. She is currently pursuing an MFA in Creative Writing and Environment at Iowa State University. Her work has appeared in or is forthcoming from *Columbia College Literary Review*, *Cold Creek Review*, *Rust + Moth*, *Buck Off Magazine Up the Staircase Quarterly*, and *Ghost City Review*. In her free time, Kate enjoys trail running and watching college wrestling.

ESSAY

Playing The Masters

—

Randy Steinberg

Let me begin where most stories do: in the past. My maternal grandmother was both an accomplished golfer and a skilled pianist — club champion on the links and proficient tickler of the ivories at home.

She bequeathed me a love of golf at an early age. Along with my grandfather, they played snowbird in their retirement years, migrating between Cape Cod and South Florida. I forged my swing bi-annually: in the summers beneath and betwixt the sandy pines of the Cape, and, in the winters, palms replaced pines in various locations around Miami and Boca. An interest in the piano took far longer to inherit, but it too began, I realize now, in those same days.

One of my fondest childhood memories is searching for golf balls with my grandfather in the woods of Cape Cod. In Florida, where the tree line was thin, one didn't have the opportunity to ball hawk, but in 1980s Cape Cod, before the housing boom, there was plenty of thick forest — beneath those same sandy pines — in which the errant shots of golfers were to be reclaimed.

My grandparents lived on the sixth hole of the New Seabury club's inland course, and in the evenings, when the course was in repose, my grandfather and I would steal into the dusk to gather the lost hopes and shattered dreams of the high handicapper.

As we'd come and go like nocturnal hunters from a den, notes from my grandmother's piano would sweep up and down the sixth hole, which was a miracle of acoustics. The tee was raised, shooting down to a valley and then up again towards the green, a 350-yard 'V.' The home was situated just past the nadir of the hole, and musical notes flowed easily in both directions.

The mosquitos were alive and evening breezes rustled the forest, but rising above it all and onto the cooling grass of the rough, fairways, and greens, the music had little trouble heralding our departures — pockets empty — and beckoning us home, our pants and belt loops now sagging with foundlings.

For a very long time, my interest lay more in golf than piano. The irony was, for as long as I could remember, we had a piano in our home. Yet neither I nor anyone else in my family utilized it. My mother explained she kept it there so that when her mother visited it would be available for play, but for most of

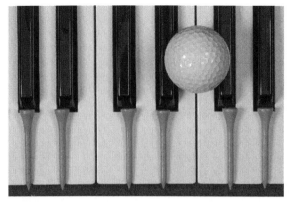

its existence the instrument — solemn, majestic and silent — gathered dust.

When I came to have a home of my own in 2010, my mother asked if I'd like the piano. I accepted, thinking it looked nice and that one day my children might learn. My two sons did not show much interest in it, and the piano continued to lie dormant until the winter of 2017-18, when I decided I needed a hobby once the golf courses closed. What would be a better choice than playing piano?

The presence of a piano in my life was ubiquitous, whether the notes floated through the Cape woods to charm me, or the instrument's physical presence was an arm's length away. The opportunity had been there; the songs had been played. But it took a long time to realize that piano and golf, for me, would be intertwined — a creeping destiny if you will.

Some people learn the piano to gain professional proficiency and to launch a career in music. Others love the challenge of setting a goal and achieving it, whether it be running a marathon or speaking a foreign language. A few think a complete life cannot be lived without competently playing an instrument. For me, there was one reason above all else (even more than having a pass time) to learn the piano: I wanted to play "The Masters."

In truth, there is no song called "The Masters"; its real name is "Augusta," composed by Dave Loggins (cousin to Kenny Loggins), and it's a tribute to Augusta National Golf Course in Augusta, Georgia, where, since 1934, one of the premier golf tournaments in the world is played every April. This tournament is known as The Masters, and its theme song, which debuted in 1982, is most often heard on television before commercial breaks. It is instantly recognizable to golfers the world over. The TV version has a guitar accompaniment which can often overshadow the piano, but when one hears it played solely on the ivories it remains singular.

The moment I decided to take up the piano, I knew instantly which song I wanted to 'master' first. I promptly signed up for lessons, telling the instructor which song I wanted to play. He asked how much time I could devote to practice. Factoring in a job and young children, I ventured a guess of about 10 minutes per day. Though he did not say anything, his expression was similar to one I might offer a beginning golfer who asks, "How long will it be before I break 80?" Nevertheless, I began my lessons, and, with only a few exceptions, have been going once per week since I commenced instruction.

A new piano student can learn one or two things in a half hour piano lesson, but practice, like most anything else is imperative, and though I have been faithful to my pledge of 10 minutes each day, I understood early on why my piano teacher had his doubts about me playing "Augusta" any time soon. I foolishly thought when I began lessons in December of 2017, I might be able to play the song by early April 2018.

To see what I faced, I printed the sheet music for "Augusta" just a few weeks after my first lesson. To the eye of a seasoned piano player, "Augusta" is probably not a difficult song to learn, but to the novice piano player, The Masters theme is a dizzying array of flats and sharps, keys I don't know how to play, and finger positions that beguile.

To play "Augusta" — or any advanced song — one has to keep both hands moving at the same time, frequently going in opposite directions or moving elsewhere on the keyboard while one hand continues steadily. Only by the first or second month of my lessons was I able to play simple tunes such as "Yankee Doodle" or "Row, Row Your Boat." By month three and four, I was playing a passable "Happy Birthday" and "When the Saints Come Marching In." I was glad for this progress, but these songs are nothing like "Augusta," which requires a variety of skills I realized might take much longer to acquire.

April 2018 quickly became April 2019, but even that estimate might have been a stretch.

As with golf, playing the piano requires perfectly timed coordination to strike the right shot or, as it were, note. Piano instruction to the beginner can be highly confusing in the same manner golf lessons are to the neophyte. A new golfer might be told to hold his or her head still, bend the knees (but not too much), keep the left arm straight, don't forget to swivel the hips, and finish with 90 percent of your weight on your front foot. And this is only a full swing. There are the dynamics and mechanics of putting, chipping, sand trap play, downhill and uphill lies, trying to move the ball right or left, and a number of other particulars a player must master to be competitive in the game.

As a long-time golfer, many of the fundamentals of the game are second nature to me, but with the piano I am the beginner, staring at a 420-yard par four with water on the right and woods on the left. I feel the psychic pain so many describe about golf, only now it is the piano and all its difficulty that tests my mental limits.

A sheet of piano music has more marks and information than any golf scorecard will ever have. Making your notes flow through a 'slur' or striking any given key more crisply when 'staccato' is called for are easy in isolation, but to execute these directions in the midst of a piece that also includes a number of other directions and cues is a challenge of the highest order.

Yet I persist because I believe that playing "The Masters" theme will be my only chance to *play The Masters*.

As of this writing, I am 45 years old, and a decent golfer with an eight handicap. Given work and family demands, I don't think I'll be getting much better at the game. But even if I somehow managed to lower my handicap I'll never compete in any big-time tournaments. It seems silly to state the obvious, but I'll never come close to playing at Augusta National Golf Club in The Masters tournament itself, and barring the oddity of an invite to play Augusta by a member, the only way I'll even get to see the course is by lottery.

What do I mean by this? For many golf events, one simply needs to buy a ticket to attend. Not so for The Masters, which issues coveted tournament tickets via lottery. Every year, I apply online, and, so far, every year, I have not been selected. But odds are I will one day get in via the lottery and thus be able to attend The Masters.

But let's take this a step farther: attending the tournament and playing the course are two different things. A spectator views the course and all its intricacies from outside the ropes. A gallery member will never know what it feels like to cross the stony bridge over Rae's Creek at the 12th hole. A spectator can see and smell the azalea and dogwood that famously grace the course, but what would it be like to stand right next to it, and — pray it does not happen — have to hunt around in it should a poor shot find its cover? What would it be like to stroll up the 18th fairway, the gallery staring back at you and the course challenging you to find the elevated green with a suitably spun ball that remains on the good side of the slope? A visitor could never perceive these sites and sensations. Only a player can.

And here is where a leap of faith or perhaps, better put, a flight of fancy, takes hold. If, one day, I can achieve a competent rendition of "Augusta," it will be as if I am playing the course itself. Making that jump in transposition on the keyboard will be like playing Amen Corner (the nickname of holes 11, 12, and 13) without a bogey or much worse. Hitting the sharps and flats correctly — while not breaking tempo — will be akin to landing in the pine straw… and escaping with a low screamer to put myself in position for a try at an up and down par save. Just being able to get through the four-page piece without a flub will be like playing Augusta and breaking 100.

And dare I go further by saying that learning The Masters theme song will be a feat greater than actually playing the course, and playing it at par or better?

Do I risk offending golf purists by declaring that if I play "Augusta" with competency I will transcend what any player has ever done? Even the greatest. Nicklaus. Palmer. Woods. Spieth. They've all won marvelous Masters' victories, but have any of them made music? Have any of them *played The Masters?*

How can I make such a claim? The answer: music is alchemy, sublime if you will, and golf profane. This is not to say golf isn't a special game for me. Of course, it is, but golf — or sport in general — as beautiful and entertaining (and frustrating) as it can be, is not the same as music.

One can play the game of golf with mastery and do things no one else can, which inspires awe, but, golf, even when played at the loftiest levels, does not create anything of a higher order. Two inert chemicals, if combined, evolve into something new — whether good or bad. Shine light through water and you get the prismatic magic of a rainbow. One musical note on its own is almost formless, but arrange several in a certain way and you transcend. As much as I love golf, I recognize there is no such analogy available that would make it more than the game it is.

But the composer or the performer of music takes individual sounds and fuses them to stir the ear and brain. Such will be my triumph over the greats of the game if I can play the song. They have mastered the base metal that is the course, but I will have taken pedestrian parts and made gold by mastering the song.

Perhaps I'm getting carried away with my aspirations. After all, we're talking about playing a popular tune on the piano. Should I be making anything more of this? There might be the personal pride of acquiring a new skill and showing it off, if not for others than just myself, but is it ridiculous to believe learning "Augusta" is anywhere close to stepping into the shoes of the game's immortals?

Whatever the answer, I keep the sheet music for "Augusta" perched upon my piano as a reminder of my goal, and I often think back to those days on Cape Cod, in the woods. The golf course. The piano. The evening breezes. A song and that creeping destiny closer to being fulfilled.

———

Randy Steinberg has a master's degree in film/screenwriting from Boston University. He taught screenwriting at BU from 1999-2010. Since 2011, he has reviewed films, television shows, DVDs, and books for *Blast Magazine.com*. He is currently developing a feature-film script with a New York City production company. This is his third *Sport Literate* essay. He lives in the Greater Boston area.

POETRY

Song for a Practice Field

———

Jeffrey Alfier

Sierra Vista, Arizona

There's a hobo camp in a thicket
of blackthorn and mesquite
between the Northrup Grumman plant
and a park where today my grandson
and I toss a glider, and my daughter's
ball team takes the practice field,
shagging flies and grounders
to tag ghost runners out.
The glider has its own play — going foul,
grabbing wind from nowhere
to arc over a toddler who glances upward
at its white wings before it drops
toward the thicket, spent like breath
in the winter air, closing with its shadow
in a clearing of buffelgrass.
And back on the field,
someone keeps screaming to hit the cutoff man.

———

Jeffrey Alfier's recent books include *Fugue for a Desert Mountain, Anthem for Pacific Avenue,* and *The Red Stag at Carrbridge: Scotland Poems. Gone This Long: Southern Poems* is forthcoming (2019). His publication credits include *The Carolina Quarterly, Copper Nickel, Midwest Quarterly, Kestrel, Southern Poetry Review, Poetry Ireland Review,* and *The Stinging Fly.* He is founder and co-editor of Blue Horse Press and *San Pedro River Review.*

L

ESSAY

Portrait of the Poet as a Young Fan

—

J.D. Scrimgeour

To see a ball change
To a dot on the pale blue,
To dent some red plastic seat
Over 400 feet away using just
A quick twist of the body,
A snap of the arms,
And a stick.

The October night in 1986 that the New York Mets won the World Series was the first and only time that I snorted cocaine. I had just begun my single year of graduate school at Columbia University after having gone there as an undergraduate, and in the euphoria following the Mets' victory, I partook in a few lines that were offered me by some friends who lived in the same building.

Given that I, like the whole city, was delirious, I really don't know if the cocaine had any effect, though I do recall lugging a plastic garbage bin filled with spiked punch two blocks, a feat that seems hard to fathom now. The punch was just part of the celebration on 114th Street, which had been cordoned off to traffic to allow a street party.

If the coke gave me an extra burst of energy, it wasn't enough to get me to follow through with the plan my buddies and I concocted around three that morning. After hours of drinking and hooting and even a little dancing on 114th Street, one of us proposed going downtown and getting good spots for the parade the next day, and soon, after sprinting through the turnstiles, we were all on the "1" train, shimmying underneath Broadway. Sitting in the nearly empty car, we spoke a few words to each other, but then mostly just sat, the energy draining from us under the harsh light. We looked around at the open seats, we looked at our somewhat pathetic selves, slumped and sleepy, and decided to turn around. At 72nd Street, we shuffled across the platform to the uptown side and returned to the campus and our beds.

Despite our late night, we managed to wake up and get downtown for the parade the next morning. It was a brisk but sunny autumn day, and the two-and-a-half million people in the streets generated a warmth that made standing outside for a couple hours not unenjoyable: the ticker tape falling from the sky like so many torn-up term papers, the glimpse of the sunglassed-heroes between the shoulders of the people in front of you, hollering their names over the crowd because, well, because what else can you do in such a moment?

I began following the Mets in 1984, the year I stopped playing baseball myself after two mediocre years as a walk-on for the Columbia junior varsity. I was living in one of the Barnard College dorms. A girl two doors down had a small television with horrid reception, and one of the few channels that came in was Channel 9, which broadcast the Mets games. I'd borrow the TV and prop it on a chair at the side of my bed, then sit back with a beer and a book while the game unfolded in front of me.

I looked forward to the Mets games, and I even checked in on them on those nights when I went out. At the West End, the bar across the street from Columbia where Jack Kerouac and Allen Ginsberg used to carouse, I'd leave my table of friends to go to the bathroom, then, returning, I'd pause in front of the TV to watch an at bat, or even an inning, my beer warming back at the table.

A devoted fan in those days, I would scoot out of my classes as soon as they ended to catch the score. I recall having a late afternoon class in Philosophy Hall during a playoff game against the Houston Astros. Someone had a little transistor radio, and before the class started I huddled in the hallway with several other students and professors, listening to the play-by-play.

I liked the Mets so much that one April day in 1985 I decided not to study for my French final exam because I didn't want to leave an extra-inning game against the Pirates. The game eventually went for 18 innings, and it included several memorable moments — Mets' outfielder Darryl Strawberry hit his first career grand slam in the first inning, and then the Mets didn't get a hit for the next nine innings. In the 9th and 12th innings, the Pirates loaded the bases with no one out, yet failed to score. Both those times, the Mets brought the entire outfield in to play behind the infielders. I remember the oddness of all those players crowded around the infield and, behind them, the empty expanse of green.

The game also featured the curious sight of two reserve outfielders, Rusty Staub and Clint Hurdle, shifting from left to right field, depending on the batter (they made the cross-outfield trek 11 times). Staub, a chunky 41-year-old, had never been fast, and he had been put on the team's roster exclusively for pinch-hitting. Still, he made a fine running catch in the 18th inning — or, as one sportswriter put it, "Well, for Staub it was 'running.'"

Sacrificing my French grade for the Mets signaled a new direction that my life was starting to take. I associated the Mets with the new, the possible. In my own life, the freshness of promise was my new discovery: poetry. My junior year, the year I watched that 18-inning game, was also the year that I began to write poetry.

Writing poetry may have been the first time in my life that I felt able to fuse the emotional and intellectual. One of my first poems, predictably, was about my grandmother, who had died the previous summer. I woke in the middle of the night in my dorm room and, not quite knowing why, scrawled the first draft. Over the next few days, I labored over the lines, selecting a word that would resonate with those in a previous stanza, playing with the line breaks to capture the pacing of speech. A few months and a few poems later, I took my first creative writing class; it's hard to believe, but that was the first class I had ever looked forward to, the first class that seemed like it had a whiff of life, of the world, in it. Writing, like baseball, or sex, was something I actually wanted to do.

Perhaps I had to stop playing baseball to discover poetry. Perhaps the concentration that I brought to each pitch while in the batter's box, the focus that I had in the field when the pitcher wound up, the little half step toward the plate to get my body moving as the batter swung, all that transferred to the act of selecting the right word or phrase, of sharpening my attention to the possibilities of the next line.

And perhaps I needed the Mets to nudge me into my adult life, one that I would craft for myself; if they could win the World Series, I could be a poet. The Mets who won the World Series felt like something new and revolutionary. They were cocky. Although they hadn't won anything, at the beginning of 1986, Davey Johnson, their manager, said that he wanted the team not just to win, but to dominate. They were a team that got into brawls and bean ball wars.

During those years I wrote a number of poems featuring the Mets. One was an ode to Strawberry, a celebration of his audacious swing. Another was written after the Mets won the World Series, and it was built around the refrain, "The Mets won the World Series!"

The Mets also helped get me over my class anxiety. My family wasn't poor, and my parents were educated, but I was at Columbia thanks to Pell Grants and other financial aid. My work-study job consisted of wearing a hair net and waiting on other students in the University's dining halls. Attending Columbia, I had suddenly been thrust into conversations about boarding schools, European vacations and cocaine; at an orientation session, I found myself in a group of students bitching about which Ivies had rejected them.

Rooting for the Mets nourished my democratic sympathies. I'd listen to conversations about last night's game among the cafeteria workers — all of them black — as my classmates requested their entrees and I served them. Or I'd talk about the hated Cardinals with some guy on the subway who was reading the back pages of the *Daily News*. "The Mets," we could all crow together, "won the World Series!"

For me, the Mets came to symbolize something resistant to tradition, to the weight of expectations in my life. If the struggling Yankees represented the past, the Mets were the future, brash and scrappy. Their World Series victory probably helped convince me that there was a world beyond the established pathways. I didn't need to go to graduate school, to follow the rules for success, and at the end of that academic year I left school, moved back in with my parents, took up four part-time jobs, and devoted myself to writing.

The Mets players were all likeable enough, and they were players you were glad were on your team, rather than the opposition, but they didn't generate a deep affection, at least in me. There was Rafael Santana, the weak-hitting shortstop with the arm just good enough to beat runners by half a step; Wally Backman, who did what gritty, undersized second basemen did — made the plays and banged out singles; Tim Teufel, and the weird way he wiggled his butt as he set himself in the batters' box — the "Teufel Shuffle" we called it; Lenny Dykstra and his tobacco-swollen cheek; Mookie Wilson with his glorious name. The players were good, with touches of personality, but they weren't great. Even the players especially skilled at their positions, team leaders like Keith Hernandez and Gary Carter, didn't inspire awe, just appreciation. They were good at what they did, but they weren't magical.

Two Mets, though, were magical. I loved the Mets because I loved their two young stars, Dwight Gooden and Darryl Strawberry. Both made the game seem easy. Strawberry wasn't perfect. As an outfielder myself, I cringed at the awkward way he caught flyballs, his elbow raised higher than his glove, which caught the ball while pointing toward the ground. But he was already awfully good, and I knew he would just get better, with his lightning swing that shot balls out of the park as easily as if he was flicking an ant off a table. In that poem I wrote to him, I celebrated the desire to be extraordinary rather than to be a team player, to aim for immortality rather than goodness. Why settle for three singles when you might hit a ball further than anyone had ever done before?

I had been watching Gooden since he came up, a 19-year-old phenom. Because it seemed like he struck out almost everyone, he was quickly given the nickname, "Dr. K," which was shortened to "Doc." Mets' fans began hanging up a row of "K"s in the bleachers to indicate each strikeout, founding a custom that still occurs in ballparks today. Doc seemed untouchable, and, in the naiveté of youth, I assumed that I was seeing the greatest pitcher to ever play the game. If he was this good at 19, wouldn't he just get better? How could one get better? In his glorious 1985 season, in which he won 24 games and lost only four, I remember being disappointed whenever he didn't strike a batter out. He was so dominating that I found myself trying to explain his greatness to friends who had no knowledge or interest in baseball. "You've got to watch this," I'd tell them when Gooden was pitching, "this is history — unbelievable."

Gooden is featured in the book *The New York Mets: Twenty-Five Years of Baseball Magic: World Series Edition*. On the second page, across from the frontispiece, are 15 photos of Gooden, a frame-by-frame look at him winding up. Turn three pages, and there's Gooden again, on the title page, curled after having just thrown a pitch, his body removed from a photo so that it's just him against the blank white of the page.

It was as if the page was looking forward, into some undefined, glorious place where Gooden, and the Mets, were headed. He had become the Mets, the fruition of 25 years, the unbelievable future. Plucked from the background, floating in the blank white, he seemed as timeless as poetry.

Of course, the Mets glory was short-lived, brought down in part by cocaine, that substance I had tried that October night. The book featuring Gooden came out in March of 1987, the same month Gooden first tested positive for coke. As the years went on, both Strawberry and Gooden were caught using it and served suspensions. Many other Mets used coke, too. Coke was probably why neither Gooden nor Strawberry had the careers that those early days promised.

Looking back, the Mets weren't especially young in 1986; it just felt that way. Hernandez, Carter, and Knight, three stalwarts, were having the final good seasons of very good careers. Other starters, like Backman, Wilson, and Santana, were in the middle of middling careers. I was the one who was young.

The year 1986, the year of triumph, the year of Mookie's ground ball and Buckner's legs and Ray Knight leaping down the third base line ecstatically, was also the year that failure was seeded. The fact that the team, which had, in fact, "dominated," during the regular season, eked out victories in the playoffs and World Series, suggested that the dominance had been a mirage, that Gooden was not the ace he seemed like he'd be, that this was a team that couldn't be carried by some megastar. This team, perhaps, was not a dynasty in the making, but a one-year wonder, like the 1984 Detroit Tigers.

Still, whether history preserves them or not, I will. The Mets came into my life the moment that writing came into my life. They made their appearances in some of my earliest poems, most of which I couldn't find if I tried. Those poems set me on the road I've traveled. That's enough, just like the memory of the Mets' glory is enough. I feel bad that Strawberry ruined a possible Hall-of-Fame career, but oh, how he seemed like he wanted to hit a home run with every swing, the longest home run ever. That's still cool.

And as for Doc? Jesus, did you see him pitch in 1985? I still have those dorm room nights, a couple of us crowding around a set, seated in a line on the bed and filling the chairs in the narrow room, including one or two dragged in from across the hall. Some drinking, lots of yammering, but when he wound up with two strikes, everyone faced the screen.

——

J.D. Scrimgeour's *Themes for English B* won the AWP Award for nonfiction. He won *Creative Nonfiction*'s Writing About Baseball contest, and he's also the author of three books of verse, most recently *Lifting the Turtle* (Turning Point, 2017). A *Sport Literate* veteran, he was featured in an online interview in March 2018.

RBIs

Alinda Dickinson Wasner

The same afternoon the Indians took the Pennant
I raced Billy Bowman toward a pop fly
That arced up out of right field
Like a missile into my eye
While a lady wearing a Cubs jacket
Shook her fist at Dad
Hollering if I hadn't been in her way
The ball would have dropped into her mitt
What could he be thinking
To drag a child to this Series anyway,
Didn't he understand this was *Cleveland?*

And though I never got to see Hank Aaron
And Rocky Colavito step up to the plate,
Later when bases were loaded
Around my hospital bed, (what with Mom on first
And Father O'Malley called in to play shortstop
At the bottom of the ninth) I drifted in and out
Of innings all my own;
But when the doctors began to argue over statistics
(one of them mentioning the word, *miracle*s,
I began to worry that the Yankees
Had won the Series after all.

By the time spring rolled around again
I'd missed most of fourth grade and story problems
But when Billy showed me his new Louisville Slugger
I knew right then I'd had enough of Barbies and backgammon
To last a lifetime
And though I hadn't intended to lie

When I promised Mom that from now on
I'd be happy with girl games,
I figured my good eye
Could still see
All that I needed to.

For hadn't I seen Mary Ellen Rivers
Get up from her hospital bed
With a metal rod screwed into her spine
And walk for the very first time?
And hadn't I seen
A boy whose brothers set him on fire
Go home with a doctor who wanted a son?
And wasn't it true
That the baby whose voice box
Was eaten away by Drano
Learned to talk with her hands?

And besides, now there were other things
To consider, such as the first breeze of April
Calling my name
And the roar of the stadium
And elephants marching down Broadway
On Channel 3 and WTAM-AMs Herb Score
Calling the plays from the radio on the the kitchen window sill:
And with Billy on second
And me stealing home
I reasoned,
What on earth could possibly go wrong?

———

Alinda Dickinson Wasner's work has appeared in *Fresh Water: Women Writing About the Great Lakes, Avatar Review, New Millennium Poets, Passages North, Wayne Review, Wittenberg Review, Blue Lake Review, Corridors, Comstock Review, UpStreet, Paint Creek Press, Outsider Writers, Corridors, Inkwell, InSpirit, The MacGuffin, Up the Staircase, Moving Out, The Detroit Free Press, Detroit Metro Times, and Michigan Natural Resources, Poetry Pacific,* and *Michigan Jewish History Journal,* and elsewhere. Her chapbooks include *Departures/Arrivals* and *Kissing The Ikons.*

L

ESSAY

The Soul of a Tigers' Fan

———

Daniel Southwell

When I was 11 I walked to the front of the church in a long line of people responding to the same call. My knees wobbled and I bowed my head when I got there, accepting the prayers. The pastor put his hands on my chest. Behind me, a deacon put his hands on my shoulders. Sweat soaked through the pastor's shirt behind his tie. They swayed and prayed and all around us people did the same. I could feel their breath and the energy pulsing off them.

When I was 18 I sat just above the bullpen at Comerica Park for a midsummer game between the Tigers and White Sox. In a pitcher's duel — 0-0 in the ninth — the crowd kept quiet because every at-bat was tense. Our newest trade stepped to the plate: some kid named Cabrera jacked a monster homer over center field to win the game in one swing. Forty thousand fans jumped up like a single organism, screaming with joy. I could feel their breath and the energy pulsing off them.

When I was 19 I drove from Michigan to Louisiana alone. I drove around the south alone, I got drunk alone, I got in fights alone. I turned 20 alone in a Motel 6 with mice and bugs in the walls. I breathed my own breaths and made my own energy.

Everything I felt, I felt for myself.

When I was 21 in Idaho, I climbed out among the deserted grain silos in the middle of the night and called my parents. When they woke up I told them about my newest breakup and cried, and they were sad along with me, but not in the same way I was. They felt something about what I was feeling, but they didn't feel what I was feeling.

I wasn't alone, but my feelings were mine alone.

Wise people warn us about the intoxication of crowds. Mobs are dangerous, and young men especially are happy to substitute belonging for conscience and reason. We've all seen religions in the news, wielding AKs, machetes, and sharpied posterboards. We've all seen sports fans flipping cars and burning neighborhoods, their celebrations and their mourning indistinguishable.

The power of feeling the same thing together is immense. It's a wordless intimacy that cuts deeper than almost anything. It's why sports are almost a religion and why religions, or the denominations within them, become competitive rivals.

It's why nations, the bastard-love children of sports and religions, can kill and rob each other.

In 2006, in rural west Michigan, it was easy to feel alone. I was 16, working 50 hours a week on a dairy farm, milking the 3 a.m. shift in a dark, deserted barn. I was poor. My family was poor. Everyone I knew was poor. The ripple-effect economic implosion that would hit the rest of the country in 2008 had already hit us hard.

I did three things other than working. I went to church. I wrote stories. And I watched the upstart Detroit Tigers scrap their way to the World Series.

I sent out stories. I got rejection letters. I pretended every rejection was fine, a badge of honor. I felt the rejections alone. I didn't know any other writers, and even if I had, writing a story is an intensely private thing, so each rejection is its own unique kind of sorrow.

At church we sang old hymns, Scottish psalter and Genevan psalter, shoulder to shoulder, as loudly as we could. Our parents filled the rows with dozens of children, and we prayed for the moral state of our nation. We felt together, as we sang and spoke in unison, that we were doing something right, something we had been made for. We felt a sturdy, warlike kind of holiness, and we felt it together, in the air around us, and we were a community.

But as the year went along, I started talking to coworkers – secular people – and I started raising my hand more at church meetings. A chip grew on my shoulder, and I looked at the outside world with more longing. Entire sermons were preached to, and about, me.

And when I stood and sang I didn't feel what they were feeling. I didn't always understand what they were feeling, and I certainly wasn't part of it.

I would stop at the gas station, or drive through the big dairy farm on a Skid-Steer and my Tigers hat caught people's eyes. We would nod to each other, and feel the same thing: a growing, cautious kind of hope. Maybe those boys who had set a record for losses in a season just three years before would do something special.

We felt like maybe something, somewhere, was going to smile on poor kicked-around Michigan working people after all.

When people saw my hat, or I saw theirs, we could launch into something deep immediately. Stats might not seem intimate. Last night's double play might not seem spiritual. But they were shorthand for something. When I asked, *Did you listen to the game last night?* I was asking, *Did you feel what I felt when Grandy threw that guy out at the plate? Did your heart sail and then falter and then go numb like mine did, when C-Mo's high fly died on the warning track?*

Ultimately I was asking, *Are you, like me, fool enough to assign feelings to things that happen to other people, way down south in Detroit, that you can't control, simply because they wear a D that says their victories and losses belong to you? Are you, like me, desperate for meaning in the middle of drudgery?*

Are you, like me, hungry to share feelings with people?

The feeling we Tigers fans ended up sharing that year was heartbreak. After barreling through the playoffs with Cinderella excitement, building a narrative of cosmic meaning in my mind, they were stomped unceremoniously by the St. Louis Cardinals.

St. Louis stole not only our hope but our narrative as the hope of the scrappy middle-Americans looking for a savior.

I wore my Tigers hat constantly in the days after, looking to share my heartbreak, and the hollowed-out looks I got from everyone I passed became in my mind a kind of brotherhood. We didn't have our World Series, but we did have our shared grief, and that was something valuable too.

The next time they went to the World Series, I was living in the panhandle of Idaho, sandwiched between Washington State and Montana, just south of Canada. I wasn't just thousands of miles away from Tigers fans, I was thousands of miles from baseball in general.

My friends knew how important the Tigers were to me, and so they watched the games with me, but they didn't feel with me. When the Giants finished massacring the Tigers and their legless bullpen, I sat alone on my kitchen floor and felt sad, but mostly I felt removed from a community. I knew that back in Michigan, everyone was grieving together.

You can only grieve so much alone.

I'm a writer, and I think stories are the most powerful thing in the world. All art, at its best, is an exercise in helping people feel what we feel, and helping them feel it together. So that's part of this conversation, too. But art is about *helping* people get as close as they can to where you're at. You're holding their hand and walking them toward feelings.

Art, at its best, is laboring to construct what sports and religion do naturally.

I still go to church, but these days it feels more like watching the Tigers alone in Idaho than it does sitting above the bullpen at Comerica Park, feeling along with a community.

It'll never feel like 2001, walking to the front of church into a haze of compounded shared feeling. I guess I'm ok with that.

I'll always be a Tigers fan. Statistically, they'll probably win it all sometime in my lifetime. But I know it'll never feel like 2006, the hope, the magic, the daring nods of "I see you" that we all gave each other during that time.

There's a lot of talk now, about the role that religion and sports play in our culture and the dangers of both. I'm glad we're talking. The danger is real. Beyond the danger of what crowds are capable of, there's the danger of ascribing too much meaning to shared feeling, to arbitrary points of happiness or grief.

But I'm afraid to lose the beauty of instant community, the shortcuts to bonding. Life is all too often lonesome, and our feelings are all too often secluded.

Let's feel things together when we can.

———

Daniel Southwell grew up in the woods of west Michigan. Besides writing, backyard sports were his main hobby. A few separated ribs and broken noses later, he became a freelance promo film writer. His personal nonfiction has appeared on Vox.com, and his fiction in the *Mysterion* anthology. He now lives in Lancaster, Pennsylvania, with his wife and two sons.

Jocks, Herbs, the '36 Yankees, Tea with Harold Bloom

—

Bill Gruber

The political columnist George Will rightly calls baseball "a thinking man's game," but the people who play it suffer nonetheless from collective misperceptions about athletes. The man who threw the pitch in Game 1 of the 1954 World Series between the Cleveland Indians and the New York Giants, the ball that the Indians' first baseman Vic Wertz blasted 420 feet to deep right center, the ball that Willie Mays somehow, miraculously, caught while running at full speed with his back turned away from the ball, was Don Liddle. The pitch Liddle threw to Wertz was hit better than any other ball that day, hit better maybe than most other baseballs on most other afternoons. Yet the box score records merely a fly ball to center. Wertz was the only batter that Liddle faced; a southpaw, he had been brought into the game in relief of Sal Maglie just to pitch to the left-handed-hitting Wertz. Following Mays' improbable catch, Liddle was immediately replaced on the mound by Marv Grissom to set up a righty-righty matchup. In the locker room after the game was over (the Giants won, 5-2), Liddle summed up his performance for his manager, Leo Durocher: "Well, I got *my* man."

Baseball players often say things like that. They are always looking at themselves and their game with a clear, ironic eye. Their humor — it is, characteristically, humor of the droll, self-deprecating variety — is unmatched by players in any other sport. Yet Arnold Hano, in his book about that catch and that game (*A Day in the Bleachers*), discredits the anecdote. Of Liddle's witticism, Hano writes: "I doubt he said it, but it makes a nice story."

Why would Hano think that? Why would he assume that someone who played baseball well enough to make a living at it would likely be too dull to make such a joke at his own expense? Intellect and baseball talent have never been proved to be mutually exclusive, but assumptions like Hano's are widespread in art and life. Take Ebby Calvin "Nuke" LaLoosh (the name itself is meant to sound foolish), a slow-witted pitcher, played by Tim Robbins, in the otherwise credible film about minor league baseball, *Bull Durham*. Kevin Costner plays Crash Davis, LaLoosh's catcher. Davis, in contrast to his pitcher, is presented as a perceptive and articulate man, but the unspoken premise of the film seems to be that above-average intelligence is generally accompanied by below-average, minor league talent.

Or remember Mark Harris's classic baseball novel, *The Southpaw*? Harris sets his story in mid- 20th century; the story is told by a pitcher named Henry Wiggen. The narrative is full of passages like this one:

> We scored in the ninth, but not enough, and Pop pumped my hand for the job I done, and the batboy brung me my street shoes and I snatched them and told him to go on about his business and not be getting in everybody's hair, and me and Pop went in Jack Hand's office under the stands and picked up our pay. Jack called me back and I said I had took the wrong envelope, and he give me another containing 2 fivers instead of the usual 1.

Harris's diction is as phony as a three-dollar bill, its style as mannered as John Lyly's 16th-century *Euphues*. If you doubt that such fictional speech abuses reality, listen to the tapes of Lawrence Ritter's interviews with more than several dozen men who played baseball in the early decades of the 20th century — Rube Marquard, Fred Snodgrass, Chief Meyers, Bill Wambsganss, and the rest. Ritter transcribed and edited the interviews for his well-known book, *The Glory of their Times*. Hearing or reading the players' recollections, the thing that strikes you most is their thoughtfulness. These are — and must always have been — intelligent, reflective men. Many of them in fact had a good deal of education for the era in which they played baseball, the first several decades of the 20th century. And even those players who lacked much formal schooling speak in Ritter's tapes as if they are fully alert to the mysteries and beauties of life and can state them clearly, sometimes eloquently. Take Sam Crawford, who described to Ritter how he spent his retirement days: "I read a lot," he says. "My favorite writer is Balzac."

Wow. When I heard Crawford say that you could have knocked me over with a feather boa. Honoré de Balzac (1799-1850) was one of the great French novelists of the mid-19th century, but I doubt that in the 1960s, when Ritter's interviews took place, you would have found many Americans — even college graduates — who knew who Balzac was, let alone who read him habitually. (On my desk, for example, is a copy of the 1963/64 edition of *Yale College Programs of Study*; in more than 200 pages full of course offerings for under-graduates, Balzac appears in just three advanced-level courses offered by Yale's French Department.) Sam Crawford had not even a high school education; he left school after the fifth grade and was a barber by trade when he entered professional baseball. Yet *The Southpaw* and books like it are praised for their "realism" in depicting the early game and the wit of the men who played it.

Another writer who doubts the intelligence of baseball players is Richard Ben Cramer. His biography of Joe DiMaggio (*Joe DiMaggio: The Hero's Life*) is detailed and thorough. But Cramer characterizes the men who played the game in this way: "Nobody got to the majors, or stayed, by exercise of sweet reason. This was a rough set of boys, mostly poor, uneducated, and possessed of powerful wills which they enforced by intimidation and physical dominance. Every once in a while, like a camel through the needle's eye, some college boy might arrive in the bigs."

Strong words: but let's test them against the record. In writing about DiMaggio, Cramer surely had to learn a good deal about DiMaggio's teammates, and the Yankee clubhouse in 1936 — the year DiMaggio joined the team — was hardly a rabble of uneducated thugs. The '36 Yankees carried 11 pitchers, and *seven* of them in fact were "college boys," including Johnny Broaca, who graduated from Yale, and Bump Hadley, a graduate of Brown. Ted Kleinhans, another pitcher, would also have qualified as a "college boy," even though he took a less well-traveled road to a bachelor's degree. Traugott Otto Kleinhans was born on April 8, 1899. After graduating from high school in Wisconsin, he enrolled at Concordia College, intending to follow the career of his father in the ministry. But when the United States entered the war in Europe, Kleinhans enlisted, joining the Ohio National Guard in May, 1917. He served in Europe with the 145th Infantry Regiment of the 37th Division and was severely wounded in the Meuse-Argonne campaign. It was during his military service that Kleinhans began to play baseball. He played for semi-pro teams all during the 1920s, finally breaking into organized ball with the Johnstown Johnnies late in the season in 1928. Kleinhans bounced from one minor league team to another for the next five years; after Johnstown, he played for the Cumberland Colts, the Terre Haute Tots, the Bloomington Cubs, the Greensboro Patriots, and the Atlanta Crackers. The Chicago Cubs bought his contract after the season ended in 1933, then traded him to the Phillies. Kleinhans took the mound for the Phillies on April 20, 1934, a few days after his 35th birthday; at the time he was the oldest rookie ever to have played in the majors. A month later, Kleinhans had to pack his bags again, when the Phillies traded him to the Reds, who then sold his contract to the Yankees, who released him late in 1936 after he had made 19 relief appearances for the team that season. After his stint with the Yankees, Kleinhans played for Kansas City, again for Cincinnati, and then with the Syracuse Chiefs of the International League. While with Syracuse in 1941 he enrolled in Syracuse University, intending for a second time to earn a degree. But once again the guns of war interrupted the bright college years of Traugott Otto Kleinhans. At 42, Kleinhans was too old to be sent into combat, but he was accepted for duty in medical administration and worked in the 52nd General Hospital in

Worcestershire, England. Returning to college a third time after World War II was over, Kleinhans finally was awarded his degree from Syracuse in June, 1947. Kleinhans' career is a testimonial not only to one baseball player's love of the game but also to his indefatigable — if roundabout — pursuit of the life of the mind.

The position players on the 1936 Yankees were less well educated as a group than the pitchers — only three of seventeen men had gone to college — but even among this group, the so-called college boys would first have had to queue up if they were to pass through the eye of a needle. The most famous of the Yankees' "college boys," of course, was first baseman Lou Gehrig, who completed two years at Columbia University before signing with the team in 1923. But also having some college experience among the position players were the third baseman Red Rolfe, a graduate of Dartmouth, and the backup catcher Bill Dickey (who holds, unhappily, a record as the player with the most World Series rings never actually to have played in a World Series); before entering professional baseball, Dickey had attended Little Rock College, a Catholic institution.

Ten of 28 players on that Yankees team — about 36 percent — either had graduated from college or had attended it. This level of education would have beat the general American population up until very recently (in the first decade of the 21st century, for purposes of comparison, slightly better than half of adult Americans had some college background), but for the 1930s it would have been frankly phenomenal[1]. In America in 1940 (the closest year for which I could find specific data), fewer than one in 10 people living in an urban area held a college degree, and among rural dwellers college-educated people were more than twice as scarce. These numbers tell a story quite different from Cramer's. In comparison with the crowd that assembled to watch them play in 1936, the Yankee lineup must have seemed like a Phi Beta Kappa reunion.

Many sportswriters who ought to know better also perpetuate the stereotype of the dumb baseball player. Leigh Montville in *The Big Bam* calls Yankees' manager Miller Huggins, a lawyer by training with a degree from the University of Cincinnati, "a rarity in the game, an educated man." But "educated men" were *not* rarities on baseball rosters — not even in the early days of the game, during the so-called deadball era. Harry Hooper recalled that when he joined the Boston Red Sox in 1909 — Hooper himself had a degree in civil engineering — five of the starting position players had college degrees, as had three members of the pitching rotation. This was at a time when about one person in 600 was enrolled in college. Roger Kahn pays lip service at least to pitchers' intelligence in his book *The Head Game* (subtitled "Baseball as Seen from the Pitcher's Mound"). But Kahn still seems at best merely intrigued by the possibility that there might be a ball player who was both smart *and* couth.

[1] Here is the roster for the 1936 Yankees; the list includes the names of all the men who played for the Yankees at least once during the 1936 season, as well as a summary of their educational backgrounds:

Pitchers: Johnny Broaca, graduated Yale; Jumbo Brown, no college; Lefty Gomez, no college; Bump Hadley, graduated Brown; Ted Kleinhans, graduated Syracuse (1947); Pat Malone, graduated Juniata; Johnny Murphy, graduated Fordham; Monte Pearson, graduated University of California; Red Ruffing, no college; Steve Sundra, no college; Kemp Wicker, attended North Carolina State.

Catchers: Bill Dickey, attended Little Rock College; Joe Glenn, no college; Art Jorgens (born Norway), no college.

Infielders: Frankie Crosetti, no college; Lou Gehrig, attended Columbia; Don Heffner, no college; Tony Lazzeri, no college; Red Rolfe, graduated Dartmouth; Jack Salzgaver, no college.

Outfielders: Ben Chapman, no college; Joe DiMaggio, no college; Myril Hoag, no college; Roy Johnson, no college; Jake Powell, no college; Bob Seeds, no college; George Selkirk, no college; Dixie Walker (the younger), no college.

More than a third of the 1936 Yankees had graduated from college or attended it. To test whether that particular team might have been extraordinary and therefore atypical with respect to major league baseball players' educations in the early decades of the 20th century, I chose on a whim two earlier teams, the 1913 Pittsburgh Pirates and the 1924 Boston Red Sox, and did a quick check on the players' schooling. On the 1913 Pirates' roster, six of 14 pitchers and seven of 23 position players had been to college, slightly more than 35 percent. As a team, in other words, the 1913 Pirates were just as well educated as the 1936 Yankees. The Red Sox of 1924 carried fewer college-educated players — five of 16 pitchers, only one of 17 position players, or just over 18 percent of the total number of men on the roster. But "college boys" were still present on that Red Sox team in *far* greater numbers than would have been the norm at the time for the general American population.

"[I]n truth," he writes, the great majority of early-twentieth-century major leaguers were ill schooled. Some were illiterate. Many of the greatest players — like Rube Waddell and Ed Delahanty — were drunks."

Kahn is right in one respect. There were surely many sinners among early baseball players, even as there were some saints (Christy Mathewson comes to mind), and the majority of both groups were probably ill-schooled. But the great majority of early-20th-century Americans were *themselves* "ill-schooled," by modern standards at least, and doubtless some of them were also illiterates or drunks. In 1910, for example, only about 9 percent of Americans possessed a high school diploma, which by modern standards makes the remaining 91 per cent of the population "ill-schooled." I can speak here not just from statistics but from personal experience. My grandfather on my mother's side of the family was born in 1884 and left school after the eighth grade; he read a newspaper daily, but in the 20 years I knew him I never saw him read anything else. My paternal grandfather's formal education was similarly limited. He was a blacksmith by trade, and, so my father often told me, drank heavily. Farmers would come to his shop needing their horses shod or their machines repaired, and when the work was done they would pay my grandfather and offer to stand him a round of drinks. Usually several rounds. Martin Luther Gruber was a drunkard until middle age, when with courage and an effort of will for which I will be forever grateful, he foreswore alcohol for the rest of his life in order to save his job and his family.

Misperceptions about athletes sometimes create their own cultural realities. My son was not a recruited athlete in college; he made the Yale baseball team as a walk-on. But even with sterling academic credentials, he told me that he routinely tried to hide from his teachers his status as a varsity athlete. One coach's advice to the players on this subject was blunt: "For God's sake, don't tell them you're a baseball player." Still it was impossible for my son to masquerade as a "Herb," a term that the players, who were themselves disrespected universally as "jocks," sometimes mockingly called non-athletes. Each spring at the start of preseason games, Yale's team coaches sent letters to faculty and residential college deans with the names of athletes who would sometimes need to miss classes to participate in a scheduled game. The baseball coaches would overlook players' late arrivals to afternoon practices because of academic commitments. (In fact, Yale's athletes' *Handbook* forbad coaches from requiring students to miss class to attend a practice.) But bus trips for games in places like Baltimore, Ithaca, or Hanover always caused absences. Even harder on players' academic schedules were the games that had to be made up because of foul weather. (March and April in New England are notoriously unfavorable to baseball.) Faculty especially begrudged the ballplayers these unanticipated absences, perhaps because they had no authority to forbid them. One week in

April of my son's last playing season, Yale's team was compelled by Ivy League Conference directors to stay through Monday in Hanover, New Hampshire, to make up two games with Dartmouth that had been rained out the previous Saturday. My son emailed the teacher of his seminar in poetry to inform him of the snafu, but the man was so certain that he was being lied to that he ordered one of his graduate assistants make repeated phone calls to the Yale Athletic Offices to verify that my son was telling the truth. My son heard about the phone inquiries subsequently and only indirectly, in conversation with a friend who worked a scholarship job in the college athletic office.

But let me close with a different story about baseball and a member of the faculty of Yale University. At the end of his sophomore year, on the recommendation of his French teacher, my son was assigned scholarship employment for the next two years working for the legendary literary critic Harold Bloom. The job was a lagniappe for my son, an English major, and for me, as Yogi Berra had once said, it was "déjà vu all over again." I myself had been an undergraduate at Yale 40 years before, and in the fall of 1964 along with two dozen other English majors I had sat in thrall as a young Harold Bloom opened up for us the sensual luxuries of John Keats' Odes or the intellectual depths of William Blake's deceptively simple couplets. The physical location in which all this played out — some nondescript classroom in W. L. Harkness Hall whose number, floor, and decor I no longer recall — I remember in only the vaguest outlines. Monday, Wednesday, and Friday mornings, Bloom simply materialized before us, emerging through a doorway, furiously tugging at the knot on his tie as if the thing were cutting off breath. It sounds silly now to say it, but as an undergraduate I had never pictured Harold Bloom in any other setting. I did not — or, for some reason, could not — think of him eating, walking, driving a car, or in any manner inhabiting a place with dimensions or solidness. When Bloom walked through that door, it no more occurred to me to wonder where he had come from than as a child I would have pondered the prior whereabouts of a department store Santa Claus. In my mind, he belonged instead to some pristine theatrical realm.

In after years I had brushed against the spell of Harold Bloom in a number of ways. In graduate school I had made use of the early interpretive books, *Shelley's Mythmaking* and *The Visionary Company*, and later, myself a professor of English, I read first his theories on the wellsprings of poetry — *The Anxiety of Influence*, *A Map of Misreading* — and later the avalanche of books in defense of writers and reading. I had heard the apocryphal stories that Bloom never brought a textbook to class because he could teach any poem entirely from memory, and I had heard the jokes, too, about his prodigious literary output: *Caller: May I speak to Harold Bloom? Voice: I'm sorry, he's busy writing a book. Caller: I'll hold.* In all those years it had never occurred to me that I might one day sit down to tea with Harold Bloom, but time and chance weave strange designs, and so one day early in May of 2008, there we were in the living room of a wood-frame house on Linden Street, my son and I and Harold Bloom, sipping Earl Grey tea, talking poetry and baseball. That a mythic figure from the past was now seated opposite me, within reach, was more than a little astonishing.

At first it was just a soft spring evening in New Haven. There was conversation about poets, about Hillary Clinton's and Barack Obama's presidential primaries, and about the Yankees' prospects for the upcoming season (it would be the first year since 1993 that the team did not make the playoffs), and Harold Bloom was so chatty and so gracious that after a short while it began to seem to me not at all extraordinary to be again in the city of my college years, seeing and hearing a ghost come out of the long ago. Then Bloom began to tell about the day he saw his first baseball game. To celebrate his sixth birthday, he said, his father had taken him to Yankee Stadium. Everybody remembers that first trip to a major league ball park, and at first Harold Bloom's tale sounded no different from mine or my son's or a thousand others — the excitement of anticipation, the tumult of the crowd, the darkened, inner tunnels and then the epiphany of the great, green sward. Only, Bloom kept reciting the names of the players. Some I recognized immediately from Yankee lore — what baseball fan hasn't heard of Lou Gehrig, Tony Lazzeri, or Frankie Crosetti? But other names were unknown to me (Jake Powell? George Selkirk?), and I was unable to follow the line of his narrative until he got to Joe DiMaggio, saying, by way of afterthought, "of course, he was playing left," and it was then that I understood what Harold Bloom was doing, what he had in fact been doing all along: he was calling out the starting lineup of the 1936 Yankees as the team streamed out of the dugout and took up defensive positions on the field. In his imagination Bloom had gone back fully to that game and that day. He was seeing the players one after another, reciting their names from memory as faithfully as he might recite the words of a beloved poem. *My God*, I thought, *he remembers it all*. The spell was complete. I was 19 again, back in Harkness Hall, awestruck.

Later that day, buttoning up my suitcase in the motel room for the return drive to Atlanta, the aura of that moment in Harold Bloom's parlor seemed already to be dissolving. I began to wonder if it might all have been illusory. Maybe Bloom had made it up? It wouldn't be the first time, I thought, that an old man invented key events of his life. So I tuned up my laptop to check the out the facts, and here is what I found: Harold Bloom was born in New York City on July 11, 1930. Exactly six years later, July 11 fell on a Saturday. The Yankees' schedule for the baseball season of 1936 had them at home in the Bronx that afternoon, playing the Cleveland Indians. The weather forecast, as published in the *New York Times*, was fair and continued warm; it must have been a perfect day in the city for fathers and their young sons to take in a ball game. You can probably guess the rest, but for the record, here it is: the box score for July 11, 1936, shows George Selkirk playing in right, Jake Powell in center, and a brand-new prospect — in time, the 21-year old rookie would become immortalized as Joltin' Joe DiMaggio, with Willie Mays, one of the two greatest center fielders of all time — stationed over in left.

———

Bill Gruber is emeritus professor of English at Emory University where he teaches an online course in baseball and American culture. He's the author of several academic books and two works of nonfiction (*On All Sides Nowhere*, Houghton Mifflin 2002, Bakeless Prize) and *Baseball in a Grain of Sand* (McFarland 2018), named a finalist for the Casey Award for the best baseball book of 2018. He lives, writes, and works at restoring a 1967 Land Rover in Moscow, Idaho. For conversations on baseball or on Series Land Rovers, email him at wegrube@emory.edu.

A chapbook from Pint-Size Publications

Photo by Brian McKenna

This Loss Behind Us
A Triple Play of Poetry
Jack Bedell \ Paul Hostovsky \ MK Punky

A *Sport Literate* original, orginally sold for $15 a pop.
Now, yours for $12 (shipped free).

Buy online: **www.pintsizepublications.com**

What's Your Story?

We can handle your truth

WHO'S ON FIRST

This first-person essay begins each issue. Mark Wukas led off "Spring Eats 1997" with "Running With Ghosts," an essay subsequently recognized in the *Best American Sports Writing* (BASW) anthology. Michael McColly's "Christmas City, U.S.A." won a creative nonfiction award from the Illinois Arts Council back in the day. Frank Soos was recognized in *BASW* in 2013 for his lead-off essay, "Another Kind of Loneliness." Most recently, *BASW 2017* gave a nod to Laura Legge's essay, "The Responsible Player."

SL Travel

As that stranger in a strange land, what did you learn on the road? What's the leisurely life like over there? Robert Parker's travel piece, "The Running of the Bull," was recognized in *Best American Essays (BAE) 2006*.

PERSONAL ESSAY

We're hip to all the nonfiction forms—nature writing, immersion journalism—whatever floats your prose. Several *Sport Literate* writers have been cited in the annual *BAE* and the *BASW* collections. Mark Pearson's essay, "The Short History of an Ear," was our first to make the latter anthology's pages. Cinthia Ritchie's "Running" appeared there in 2013. Last year, Michael J. Hess earned recognition from *BAE* for his *SL* essay, "On the Morning After the Crash." Just prior to this printing, Liz Prato scored a twofer "Best American" nod with recognition in both anthologies for "Flights of Two," an essay we published in 2017

———

POETRY

Frank Van Zant handles the poetry. You mighte peruse the verse here and take in a back issue or two. Send up to three at a time our way, and we'll get it to Frank.

———

INTERVIEWS

We hope these are just good conversations with smart people. In past issues, we've featured Chicago footballers (Bear, Chris Zorich, and Cardinal, Marshall Goldberg), sportswriters (Bill Gleason and Robert Lipsyte), and even a poet (Jack Ridl). Query with suggestions.

———

SL SHORTS

In our "20th Anniversary Issue," we offered 11 quick hits of flash nonfiction. In a contest judged by Dinty W. Moore, Robert Wallace took home the $500 prize for his short, "Rush Lake." We'd like to keep it going. Send us your clean shorts (meaning crisp and properly proofed) of 750 words or less.

All submissions come online now through
Submittable on our website.

www.sportliterate.org

Frank Robinson, 1956

Jerry Judge

Blasted from your bat -
opposite field dingers
into Crosley Field's Moondeck.
Hidden power, pure force of will.

Crouched over plate, pitcher's
duty to tickle your chin.
Again, again in vain.
An inch you never budged.

A rookie among veterans —
Big Klu, Wally Post, Gus Bell.
Only you played with a fire
that scorched the devil in hell.

Jerry Judge has had seven poetry collections published and many poems in journals and anthologies. He's a past president of the Greater Cincinnati Writers League and currently facilitates the poetry group for Cincinnati Writers Project. Though he says he suffers with the misfortunes of the Bengals and Reds, he nevertheless rejoices in the success of Xavier and University of Cincinnati basketball teams.

Billy with Kite
The cover photo comes from one of our favorite poets, Jeffrey Alfier. He caught his grandson here in the same Arizona ballpark that serves as the setting for his poem, "Song for a Practice Field," which you'll find in our baseball section.

Made in the USA
Middletown, DE
26 July 2019